Professional Library
Oaklawn Psychiatric Center
2600 Oakland Ave.
Elkhart, IN   46517

D1198082

SUBSTANCE ABUSE:

THE NATION'S NUMBER

ONE HEALTH PROBLEM

Key Indicators for Policy

Prepared by

INSTITUTE FOR HEALTH POLICY, BRANDEIS UNIVERSITY

for

THE ROBERT WOOD JOHNSON FOUNDATION

PRINCETON, NEW JERSEY

October 1993

616.86

Principal Investigator
  Constance Horgan

Co-Principal Investigator and Lead for Overview and Section 1
  Mary Ellen Marsden

Co-Principal Investigator and Lead for Sections 2 and 3
  Mary Jo Larson

Project Coordinator
  Elsa A. Elliott

Other Brandeis Staff
  Sherry Angelo, Helen L. Batten, Francis Buckley, Julie Buckley, Susan Hogan,
  Lucinda Frode, Margaret Lee, Mark Plume, Michele Rountree, Linda Wastila

Editorial Consultant
  Jane Stein

The Robert Wood Johnson Foundation Project Director
  Dianne C. Barker

The Robert Wood Johnson Foundation Editorial and Production Staff
  Victoria D. Weisfeld, Joan K. Hollendonner, Linda G. Baker, Jeanne M. Weber
  with editorial assistance from Nancy Kaufman, Marjorie Gutman

Book & Chart Design
  The Barnett Group, Inc.

  Institute for Health Policy
  Heller Graduate School
  Brandeis University
  415 South Street
  Waltham, MA 02254-9110

  The Robert Wood Johnson Foundation
  College Road
  P.O. Box 2316
  Princeton, NJ 08543-2316

  ISBN 0-942054-08-3

TABLE OF CONTENTS

ACKNOWLEDGEMENTS

WE WOULD LIKE to thank a number of people who provided very helpful advice on aspects of this report, including the overall organization and content, the list of indicators, and locating data sources. The following people served on our Advisory Board: James J. Collins, John S. Gustafson, Michael Klitzner, Patrick M. O'Malley, Peter Reuter, Nancy Rigotti, and Robin Room. Also helpful were government officials who served in an ex-officio capacity on the Advisory Board: Zili Amsel, Ann Blanken, Richard Fuller, Gary A. Giovino, Thomas Harford, Gale Held, Jerome Jaffe, and James Kaple. Dorothy Rice provided special cost calculations, and data also were provided by Rosanna Coffey, Joseph C. Gfroerer, Thomas Novotny, and Fred Stinson. Additional reviewers from Brandeis University were Deborah Garnick, Jeffrey Prottas, and Arthur Webb. Each provided useful advice on the most recent data sources as well as on accurate interpretation of data.

C.H., M.E.M., M.J.L.

PREFACE

IMPROVING THE HEALTH and health care of the American people is the mission of The Robert Wood Johnson Foundation. As a national philanthropy, the Foundation supports projects that provide services, conduct research and training and a range of other activities that we hope will have an impact beyond our grantees' efforts: New models of care are tested so that others may adopt the most promising ones; health care leaders are trained so that they may discover new approaches and, in turn, influence the next generation.

Policymaking takes place on many levels, with the participation of many people—business and community leaders, legislators, health professionals, interest group representatives, and voters. All have a role to play. Through the publication of a series of policy-relevant reports, the Foundation hopes to strengthen the ability of those participants to play effective roles in the decision-making process, by arming them with simple, yet critical indicators that quickly summarize the nation's progress regarding specific health policy issues. Tracked over time, these indicators also can serve as early warning signals, alerting policymakers to future problem areas.

Each report in the current indicator series describes one of the four health policy areas chosen by the Foundation as major program goals for the 1990s:
▶ assuring access to basic health care for all Americans;
▶ improving the way services are organized and provided to people with chronic health conditions;
▶ promoting health and preventing disease by reducing harm from substance abuse; and
▶ seeking opportunities to help the nation address the problem of escalating medical costs.

Once our authors constructed a conceptual framework to measure each area, indicators were selected based upon their policy-relevance, the availability of data, and their ability to highlight a specific point and contribute to an overall understanding of the area.

We hope this report will serve as a helpful resource, and we encourage readers to share its information with others. If you have comments or suggestions, we would like to hear from you, as we decide whether subsequent editions would be useful. Please tell us what you think.

STEVEN A. SCHROEDER, MD
President

ABOUT THE TERMS USED IN THIS REPORT... The labels used in this report for population groups, risk groups, and health problems are those used by the original data sources. In some cases, these labels—ethnic and racial identities are a good example—reflect old values. We adopted this approach, despite our desire to be sensitive to changing preferences, because of the lack of consensus about which terms are preferred and to avoid potential confusion when people go back to an original data source to learn more about an issue.

CAUTIONARY NOTES FOR DATA INTERPRETATION... This report presents data on trends in substance use, consequences, and intervention efforts, as well as comparisons among subgroups of the population on these issues. In most cases, available information was not sufficient to test for statistical significance of differences between years or between subgroups. Accordingly, caution should be exercised in comparing the magnitude of such differences. In addition, trend data are generally drawn from cross-sectional surveys or other data that do not represent the experience of the same individuals over time. Despite these cautionary notes, the consistency of long-term trends and evidence from several sources is supportive of the major conclusions discussed here about the magnitude of the substance abuse problem and progress made in combatting it.

OVERVIEW: THE CONTEXT OF SUBSTANCE ABUSE

A S THE NUMBER *one health problem in the country, substance abuse places a major burden on the nation's health care system and contributes to the high cost of health care. In fact, substance abuse—the problematic use of alcohol, illicit drugs and tobacco—places an enormous burden on American society as a whole. It can harm health, family life, the economy and public safety, and it threatens many other aspects of life as well. Substance abuse affects all segments of society, but it disproportionately affects disadvantaged groups and threatens the future of young people.*

► There are more deaths, illnesses and disabilities from substance abuse than from any other preventable health condition. Of the two million U.S. deaths each year, more than one in four is attributable to alcohol, illicit drug or tobacco use. Many of these deaths and other losses could be reduced—if not eliminated—by changing people's habits.

Alcohol and illicit drug use can result in family violence and maltreatment of children, and the loss of a family member due to substance abuse has lifelong ramifications. Passive smoking causes respiratory problems in children and adults. The workplace is affected as well. Alcohol and drug abusers are costlier, less productive employees. Millions of people are arrested for driving under the influence of alcohol or drugs and for other crimes related to alcohol and illicit drug use. The safety of many neighborhoods—and the people living and working in them—is threatened by violence associated with drug sales.

Federal, state, and local governments, as well as private citizens' groups, have acted to counter the enormous societal impact of substance abuse, but much remains to be done. A great deal of the harm associated with substance abuse can be prevented with increased public awareness of the problem and concerted public action. One step in this direction is the spread of effective prevention programs throughout the country with widespread support from community groups, business and private citizens.

USE, ABUSE AND DEPENDENCE...Many people who drink, take illicit drugs or smoke occasionally do not experience problems from using these substances (although it is possible to have a serious injury or even to die from a single episode of alcohol or drug use). However, with heavier, more frequent consumption, they are more likely to experience problems with health, family members and other people, school, work or the law. Substance abuse refers to patterns of use that result in health consequences or impairment in social, psychological, and occupational functioning. While substance abuse concerns problems in living, dependence involves compulsive use, craving, and increased tolerance.

Although it is not possible to predict who will develop problems under what circumstances, in general, more serious problems develop when people become dependent on alcohol, illicit drugs or tobacco. A person who is dependent on a substance has a great need for it—often in increasing amounts—in spite of trying to cut back. The process of becoming dependent is complex and is related to a number of factors, including the addictive properties of the substance, family and peer influences, personality and existing psychiatric disorders. Genetics also plays a role in alcohol addiction, and recent research suggests that it may play a role in tobacco addiction, as well. At this time, its role in addiction to illicit drugs is not clear.

Once a person is dependent on a substance, abuse becomes a chronic, relapsing condition characterized by waves of abuse, decreased use, and abuse again. It is very difficult to quit or curtail use, and frequently more than one attempt is needed—sometimes over a long period of time—before a person successfully quits or gets use under control. The likelihood of relapse is high.

This report presents measures of use, abuse and dependence to illustrate the magnitude of the substance abuse problem. Although the focus is substance abuse—use that has resulted in significant problems for the user—information also is presented about patterns of use and the populations at risk.

HISTORICAL TRENDS IN CONSUMPTION & POLICY...The use of alcohol, illicit drugs and cigarettes has fluctuated during this century in response to shifts in public tolerance and with various political and economic events. In recent times, smoking began to decrease in the mid-1960s, drug use in the late 1970s and alcohol consumption in the mid-1980s. Many people attribute these decreases to:
► increased awareness of the health risks posed by substance abuse;
► more governmental involvement in prevention, intervention and treatment efforts; and
► the development of grassroots efforts and community coalitions directed toward decreasing substance abuse and its negative impacts.

Alcohol... Alcohol consumption in the United States has risen and fallen over time. It was high during war years—the Civil War, World War I and World War II—and low following Prohibition and during the Depression. Consumption was the lowest in U.S. history —0.9 gallons of ethanol per person aged 14 and older—in 1934, as the Depression was at its peak, and highest at 2.8 gallons per capita—around 1980, following a period in which more than half the states lowered the legal drinking age to 18.

Historically, alcohol consumption has been higher and was perhaps double current consumption in the late 1700s and early 1800s. It fell during the heyday of the temperance movement in the mid-1800s, but it began to rise again in the latter part of the 19th century (see Chart 1). The 1919 passage of a constitutional amendment that prohibited the manufacture, transportation and sale of alcohol—also known as Prohibition—decreased use again, at least legal use, and temporarily. During this time, an underground alcohol industry flourished and drinking continued to some degree. The amendment was repealed in 1933 as concerns about lawlessness rose.

During the past decade, alcohol consumption has declined. This coincided with raising the minimum drinking age to 21 in all states to counter the alarming number of fatal automobile crashes involving alcohol and teenagers. The decrease also is related to a shift in beverage preference. The consumption of distilled spirits, which has a high ethanol content, decreased substantially over the past 15 years; beer consumption remained relatively stable; and wine consumption increased slightly. Both beer and wine have a lower ethanol content. These overall trends in current alcohol consumption mask many important differences in drinking patterns across the life course and among demographic groups, as described in this report.

Chart 1. Trends in Alcohol Use

Annual Per Capita Consumption in Gallons of Ethanol

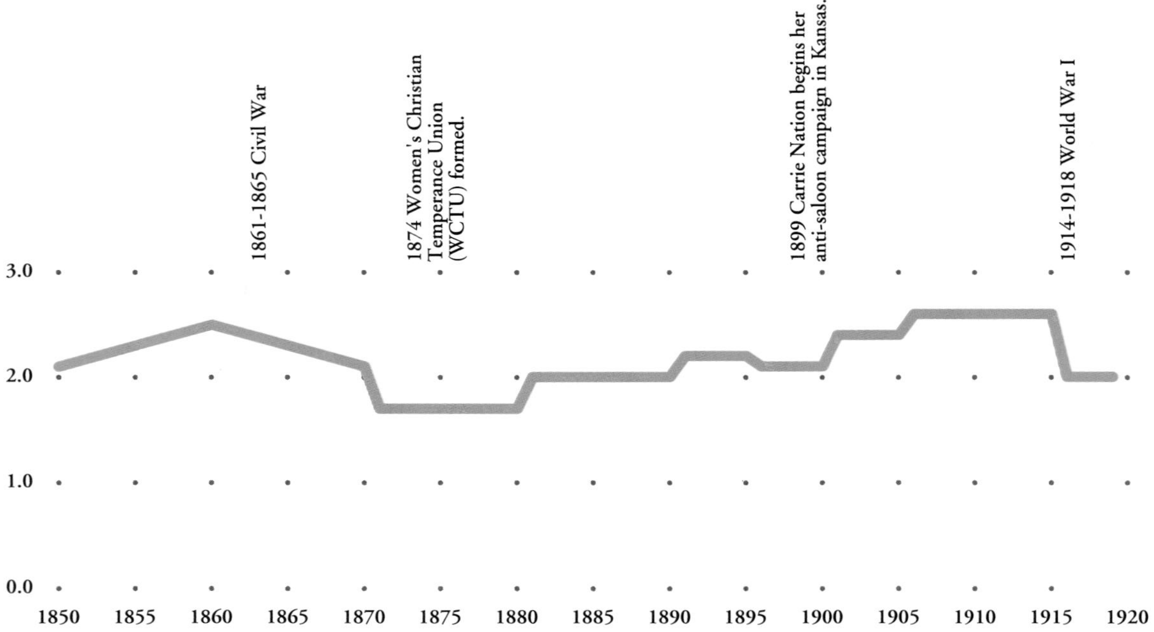

Illicit drugs... The history of illicit drug use in the United States also is marked by shifts in public attitudes and policies, between tolerance and intolerance. During the late 1800s, *laissez-faire* approaches to the problem of drug use began to be supplanted by increasing governmental regulation as the medical profession and the public became aware of the addictive properties of certain drugs. At that time, cocaine and opiates, which were inexpensive and readily available, were used widely in medicines available over the counter. A series of legislative acts and court cases during the first two decades of this century resulted in a decrease in cocaine and opiate use, and the nation's drug problem diminished during the Depression and World War II.

During the 1950s and 1960s, however, heroin emerged as a problem in our cities, and use of a variety of illicit drugs grew among the general population in the 1970s, peaking in the late 1970s for most drugs. The 1960s and 1970s also saw the development of modern treatment modalities, including methadone maintenance, therapeutic communities, and outpatient care. Illicit drug use decreased among most segments of the population during the 1980s and 1990s.

To illustrate recent trends, selected historical events are charted against recent marijuana use among 18- to 25-year olds from 1972 to 1992 and cocaine use among 18- to 25-

Notes:
Alcohol consumption is measured in gallons of ethanol (absolute alcohol) per person aged 15 and older prior to 1970 and 14 and older thereafter.

Sources:
National Institute on Alcohol Abuse and Alcoholism, Division of Biometry and Epidemiology. Surveillance Report # 23, Apparent Per Capita Alcohol Consumption: National, State, and Regional Trends, 1977-1990. *December 1992. Table 1. p. 16-17.*

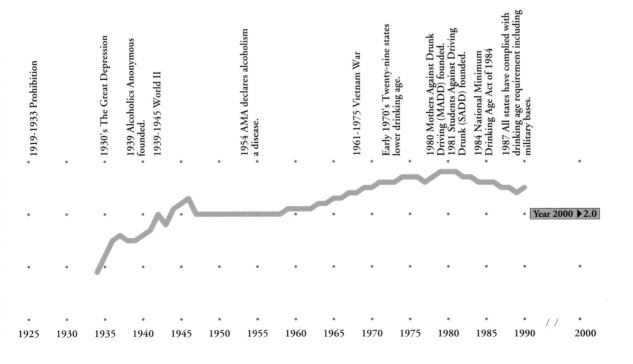

1919-1933 Prohibition

1930's The Great Depression

1939 Alcoholics Anonymous founded.

1939-1945 World II

1954 AMA declares alcoholism a disease.

1961-1975 Vietnam War

Early 1970's Twenty-nine states lower drinking age.

1980 Mothers Against Drunk Driving (MADD) founded.
1981 Students Against Driving Drunk (SADD) founded.

1984 National Minimum Drinking Age Act of 1984

1987 All states have complied with drinking age requirement including military bases.

Year 2000 ▶ 2.0

1925   1930   1935   1940   1945   1950   1955   1960   1965   1970   1975   1980   1985   1990   2000

year olds from 1974 to 1992 (see Chart 2). This age group has high rates of marijuana use. By 1979, 35 percent of 18- to 25-year olds reported being current marijuana users. This was a peak period not only for marijuana use among 18- to 25-year olds, but also for most drugs and for most age groups. Since then, marijuana use has decreased, and by 1992, about 11 percent of 18- to 25-year olds reported using marijuana in the past month. There is continued concern over the impact of illicit drug use, especially cocaine and its derivative, crack. Reported declines in frequent cocaine use since 1985 are not statistically significant. Federal drug policy has emphasized law enforcement and interdiction to reduce the supply of illicit drugs, but recent trends show an increasing interest in prevention and treatment as control measures.

Tobacco... Tobacco is a part of this land's earliest history, predating the arrival of Columbus. Native Americans had long cultivated tobacco and used it in various forms, including cigars, cigarettes, chewing tobacco, and pipes. During the 17th century, tobacco began as an important cash crop for North Carolina, and by 1864 it was a significant enough commodity that a federal tax was imposed on cigarettes to help finance the Civil War. By the 1890s, cigarette machines were perfected that produced cigarettes in much greater volume than possible by hand.

Chart 2. Trends in Illicit Drug Use

Percent Marijuana and Cocaine Users Aged 18-25

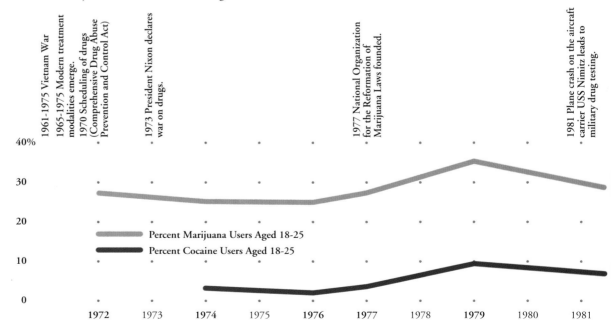

1961-1975 Vietnam War
1965-1975 Modern treatment modalities emerge.
1970 Scheduling of drugs (Comprehensive Drug Abuse Prevention and Control Act)
1973 President Nixon declares war on drugs.
1977 National Organization for the Reformation of Marijuana Laws founded.
1981 Plane crash on the aircraft carrier USS Nimitz leads to military drug testing.

Percent Marijuana Users Aged 18-25
Percent Cocaine Users Aged 18-25

40%
30
20
10
0

1972   1973   1974   1975   1976   1977   1978   1979   1980   1981

Cigarette consumption increased dramatically between 1900 and the mid-1960s, with small peaks and valleys paralleling historical events: It was slightly higher during World War I and World War II, and lower during the Depression years (see Chart 3). Consumption peaked in 1963, at 4,345 cigarettes per person aged 18 and older per year. (Smoking a pack of cigarettes a day amounts to about 7,500 cigarettes a year.) The precipitating event in the decline since then was the 1964 Surgeon General's Report that definitively linked cigarette smoking to health problems.

The tobacco industry has tried to reverse the downward trend in tobacco consumption. For example, filter cigarettes were heavily promoted during the 1950s, and low-tar cigarettes were introduced in the 1960s. Smokeless and perfumed cigarettes were introduced in the 1980s to attract new smokers and keep current smokers from quitting. The tobacco industry also has targeted minorities and women in their advertising.

In spite of these efforts, consumption continues to decline. The decreases, however, have not been uniform across all groups. The poor, the less-educated and minority groups have had smaller reductions in rates, and so have women in comparison to men. While the 1992 per capita consumption was the lowest since 1963—2,629 cigarettes a person a year—it is roughly the same as in the early 1940s.

Notes:
Data for 1992 are preliminary.

Sources:
Substance Abuse and Mental Health Services Administration, Office of Applied Studies. National Household Survey on Drug Abuse: Highlights 1991. Rockville, MD: DHHS Pub. No. (SMA) 93-1979, 1993. Table A. 10, p. 78.
Substance Abuse and Mental Health Services Administration, Office of Applied Studies. Preliminary Estimates from the 1992 National Household Survey on Drug Abuse. Advance Report No. 3. Rockville, MD: June, 1993. Table 7A, p. 44.

1984 Crime Control Act increased Federal penalties for drug offenses.

1985 "Just Say No" campaign started.

1986 Athlete Len Bias dies from use of crack/cocaine.

1989 President Bush's speech on drugs.

Year 2000 ▶ 7.8%

Year 2000 ▶ 2.3%

| 1982 | 1983 | 1984 | 1985 | 1986 | 1987 | 1988 | 1989 | 1990 | 1991 | 1992 |

ALL SEGMENTS OF SOCIETY AFFECTED... No population group is immune to substance abuse and its effects. Men and women and people of all ages, racial and ethnic groups and levels of education smoke, drink and use illicit drugs. In 1991, some 103 million Americans used alcohol in the past month, 46 million smoked, and almost 13 million used illicit drugs. There are, however, significant differences in substance use among groups. Young adults, for example, are the group most likely to use alcohol, illicit drugs and tobacco, and many adolescents have already started. In terms of gender, men are more likely than women to use most substances, but they are particularly more likely to be heavy users of alcohol and to

be problem drinkers.

Whites are more likely than blacks or Hispanics to drink, but they are no more likely to drink heavily. Native Americans, meanwhile, are more apt to have problems with alcohol. Illicit drug use disproportionately affects minority groups, with minority groups at an additional risk for a range of adverse consequences, because they are more likely to use these drugs intravenously.

Level of education is increasingly recognized as an important correlate of substance use, with heavier use among those who are less well-educated. People with higher education levels are more likely to drink, but those with less education are more likely to

Chart 3. Trends in Cigarette Use

Annual Per Capita Consumption of Cigarettes

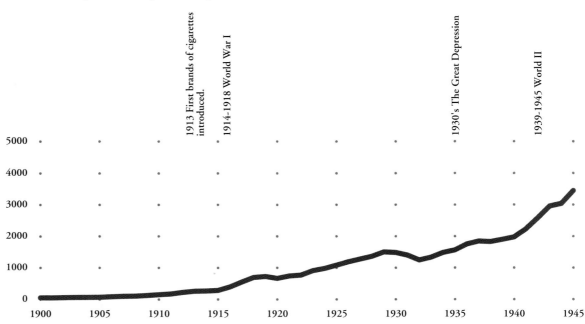

drink heavily. Among less-educated people, smoking is more common and smoking cessation less likely.

The impact of substance abuse is felt from earliest infancy through old age. Some infants are born already compromised through exposure to substances consumed by their mothers during pregnancy. Throughout childhood, boys and girls are affected in many ways by their parents' substance use, from neglect and abuse associated with alcohol and illicit drug abuse to chronic respiratory problems from environmental tobacco smoke.

Adolescence is a period of experimentation with substance use, and teenagers are particularly at risk for being involved in alcohol- and drug-related vehicle injuries. Because substance use is higher in young adulthood, men and women in this age group are more likely to experience problems associated with it. For example, workplace problems and family disruption can develop during this time. But it is later in life that the long-term health effects from alcohol use and cigarettes are most apparent. A lifetime of drinking and smoking exacts a heavy toll in chronic health problems and premature death.

SOCIETAL COSTS OF SUBSTANCE ABUSE... The total economic cost of substance abuse on the U.S. economy each year is staggering, and at least one estimate is in excess of $238

Notes:
Data for 1992 are preliminary.

Sources:
For 1900-1974:
Tobacco Yearbook 1981. *Col. Clem Cockrel. Bowling Green, KY. p.53.*
For 1975-1981:
US Department of Agriculture. Tobacco Situation and Outlook Report. *Commodity Economics Division, Economics Research Service. Rockville, MD: April 1985. Table 2, p.6.*
For 1982-1991:
US Department of Agriculture. Tobacco Situation and Outlook Report. *Commodity Economics Division, Economics Research Service. Rockville, MD: April 1992. Table 2, p.4.*
For 1992:
US Department of Agriculture. Tobacco Situation and Outlook Report. *Commodity Economics Division, Economics Research Service. Rockville, MD: April 1993. Table 2, p.4.*

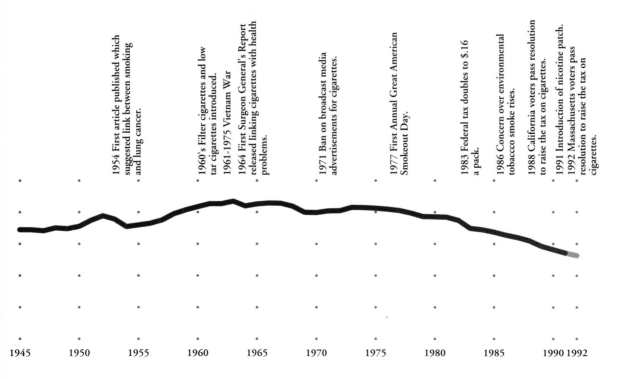

1954 First article published which suggested link between smoking and lung cancer.

1960's Filter cigarettes and low tar cigarettes introduced.
1961-1975 Vietnam War
1964 First Surgeon General's Report released linking cigarettes with health problems.

1971 Ban on broadcast media advertisements for cigarettes.

1977 First Annual Great American Smokeout Day.

1983 Federal tax doubles to $.16 a pack.

1986 Concern over environmental tobacco smoke rises.

1988 California voters pass resolution to raise the tax on cigarettes.

1991 Introduction of nicotine patch.
1992 Massachusetts voters pass resolution to raise the tax on cigarettes.

1945   1950   1955   1960   1965   1970   1975   1980   1985   1990 1992

Notes:
Medical: Direct
expenditures.
Illness: Present value of
lost productivity due to
illness or injury.
Deaths: Present value of
future lost productivity
due to premature death.
Other Related Costs:
Direct—crime, motor
vehicle crashes, etc.
Indirect—victims of
crime, incarceration, etc.
Special Conditions: AIDS
attributable to drug
abuse. Fetal Alcohol
Syndrome.

Sources:
Unpublished data for
1990 from Dorothy P.
Rice. Institute for Health
and Aging, University of
California at San Fran-
cisco, CA 94143-0612.

billion. Although specific cost estimates vary across studies because of differences in underlying assumptions and definitions, all show substantial economic costs. This is an enormous burden that affects all of society—people who abuse alcohol, illicit drugs or tobacco, and those who do not. This cost includes the expense of treating substance abuse, the productivity losses caused by premature death and inability to perform usual activities, and costs related to crime, destruction of property and other losses.

Alcohol is the most costly abused substance, with the total bill to the nation estimated to be $99 billion in 1990. Using the same economic model, the cost of drug abuse was $67 bil-

lion, and preliminary estimates place the cost of smoking at $72 billion (see Chart 4). Each substance has different impacts on users and on society. The major burden of alcohol abuse relates to productivity losses associated with illness and death; crime plays the major role in drug-related costs; and for smoking, the most significant losses are associated with premature deaths.

The core costs of alcohol and illicit drug abuse (costs of medical expenses, illness and death) fall disproportionately on people ages 15 to 44. This reflects their higher prevalence of substance abuse problems and larger number of related deaths. The core costs for most other health conditions tend to be concentrated in older age groups.

Chart 4. Economic Costs of Substance Abuse, 1990

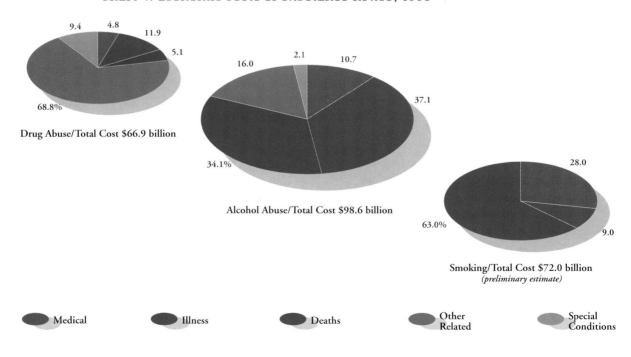

Drug Abuse/Total Cost $66.9 billion

Alcohol Abuse/Total Cost $98.6 billion

Smoking/Total Cost $72.0 billion
(preliminary estimate)

Medical   Illness   Deaths   Other Related   Special Conditions

TAKING ACTION... Substantial governmental and private efforts are being directed toward combatting the nation's substance abuse problem, and there is a clear mandate to do more. However, the sheer size of the alcohol and tobacco industries and their influence in the economy—national, state and local—impedes progress. With more than 100,000 manufacturing employees, these industries have a combined payroll that is more than 1.5 times the nation's soft drink manufacturing industry. Retail sales for beer, wine and distilled spirits total $92 billion, and tobacco sales total $44 billion. To help promote these sales, alcohol and tobacco are among the most widely advertised products in the country. In 1990, $3.9 billion was spent on tobacco advertising and promotions. Moreover, even though per capita consumption is down, profits for tobacco manufacturers increased from 7 cents per pack in 1981 to 35 cents in 1991.

These numbers powerfully influence the mix of governmental policies toward substance abuse. Some policies regulate, tax and otherwise limit the distribution of these products, while others create tax write-offs for advertising them. In addition, tobacco and alcohol advertising targets some of the very groups at which the public health community is aiming its health promotion efforts.

MONITORING CHANGE... This report presents indicators that describe the nature and extent of substance use and abuse, associated consequences, and efforts to combat the problem. Throughout, descriptive findings are provided as well as measures that document change over time. Observed increases and decreases in these indicators will help determine how successful efforts have been and where additional resources need to be targeted.

Meanwhile, the U.S. Public Health Service has set objectives for decreases in the use of alcohol, illicit drugs, and tobacco as part of a major effort to increase the span of healthy life for Americans, reduce health disparities among population groups, and achieve access to preventive services for all. The federal government's *Healthy People 2000: National Health Promotion and Disease Prevention Objectives* offers specific measurable targets across the life course and for many population groups.

The indicators presented in this report were chosen after careful review of current knowledge about substance abuse and its impact. National data were emphasized, although the charts also trace the progress of important population subgroups, such as youth. A number of the *Healthy People 2000* objectives appear within the indicators in this report, as noted. Together, the year 2000 objectives and the indicators presented here provide a blueprint for action and a means of charting our nation's progress against substance abuse.

FURTHER READING

USE, ABUSE AND DEPENDENCE

U.S. National Institute on Drug Abuse. *Drug Abuse and Drug Abuse Research.* The Third Triennial Report to Congress from the Secretary, Department of Health and Human Services. Rockville, MD: DHHS Pub. No. (ADM) 91-1704, 1991.

HISTORICAL TRENDS
IN CONSUMPTION AND POLICY

Levine, HG. "The Alcohol Problem in America: From Temperance to Alcoholism," *British Journal of Addiction,* 79:109-119, 1984.

Musto, DF. *The American Disease: Origins of Narcotic Control.* New York: Oxford University Press, 1987.

Musto, DF. "Opium, Cocaine and Marijuana in American History," *Scientific American,* July, 40-47, 1991.

Slade, J. "The Tobacco Epidemic: Lessons From History," *Journal of Psychoactive Drugs,* 21 (3): 281-291, 1989.

ALL SEGMENTS OF SOCIETY AFFECTED

Clark, WD, Hilton, ME (eds.). *Alcohol in America: Drinking Practices and Problems.* Albany: State University of New York Press, 1991.

Substance Abuse and Mental Health Services Administration. Office of Applied Studies. *National Household Survey on Drug Abuse: Main Findings 1991.* Rockville, MD: DHHS Pub. No. (ADM) 93-1979, 1993.

SOCIETAL COSTS OF SUBSTANCE ABUSE

Rice, DP, Kelman, S, Miller, LS, Dunmeyer, S. *The Economic Costs of Alcohol, and Drug Abuse and Mental Illness 1985.* San Francisco: DHHS Pub. No. (ADM) 90-1694, 1990.

TAKING ACTION

Kleiman, MAR *Against Excess: Drug Policy for Results.* New York: Basic Books, 1992.

MONITORING CHANGE

U.S. Department of Health and Human Services, Public Health Service. *Healthy People 2000: National Health Promotion and Disease Prevention Objectives.* Full Report, with Commentary. Washington, DC: DHHS Pub. No. (PHS) 91-50212, 1991.

SECTION 1: PATTERNS OF USE FAST FACTS

▸ *Americans are increasingly aware of the risks associated with substance abuse, although many young people do not believe that heavy use is really risky.*

▸ *Early use is related to later problems. By the eighth grade, 70 percent of adolescents have consumed alcohol, 44 percent have smoked cigarettes, 10 percent have used marijuana and 2 percent have tried cocaine.*

▸ *The overall use of alcohol, illicit drugs and cigarettes has decreased, but heavy use has been more stable.*

▸ *Males are three times more likely than females to be heavy drinkers and two times more likely to use marijuana frequently.*

▸ *Substance abuse is a chronic, relapsing condition: Substance abusers may be in treatment multiple times—or make repeated attempts to quit on their own—before being successful.*

PERCEPTION OF RISK

AMERICANS INCREASINGLY recognize that the use of alcohol, illicit drugs, and tobacco carries substantial health risks. And, as a result, substance use among many segments of the population has declined.

Several factors contribute to this change in the perception of potential harm (Indicator 1a). One is the success of intensive community-based and public information campaigns on the health hazards of substance abuse. Another is a greater societal commitment to healthy lifestyles in general and increased disapproval of substance use. Research suggests that at least two of these factors — increased awareness of risks and disapproval of use — have led to a drop in marijuana use among youth. Despite increases in the percent of youth perceiving great risk, the percent still falls far below the objectives targeted by *Healthy People 2000.*

Not all substances are perceived as equally risky. Illicit drug use is viewed by people of all ages as much riskier than smoking or drinking, and regular or heavier use of drugs or alcohol is seen as riskier than occasional or experimental use. There also are differences in perception of risk by age (Indicator 1b). In general, older people are more likely than young people to think that substance use is risky. One exception is that most teenagers as well as people ages 35 and older think using marijuana regularly is risky.

Cigarettes are the only substance that is perceived as increasingly risky with each successive age group. Forty-eight percent of youth think it is risky to smoke one or more packs a day, whereas 68 percent of people 35 and older believe it risky. The fact that so many young people do not think smoking is risky is especially important because youth is a period of experimentation. More information about the risks of smoking should be targeted specifically to teenagers.

Americans also are worried about environmental tobacco smoke — the exposure of nonsmokers to cigarette smoke in people's homes, at work and in public places. According to a nationwide poll, three of four nonsmokers at some point in their lives have lived with smokers, and nearly half are concerned that environmental smoke might cause serious health problems for them.

1a. What Young People Think about Substance Use

Percent of High School Seniors who Believe Substance Use is Very Risky

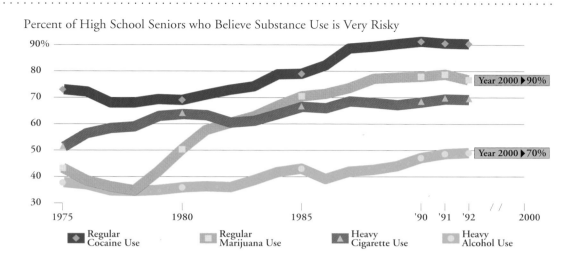

Year 2000 ▶ 90%

Year 2000 ▶ 70%

◆ Regular Cocaine Use   ■ Regular Marijuana Use   ▲ Heavy Cigarette Use   ● Heavy Alcohol Use

1b. What Americans Think about Substance Use

Percent of Americans who Believe Substance Use is Very Risky, 1991

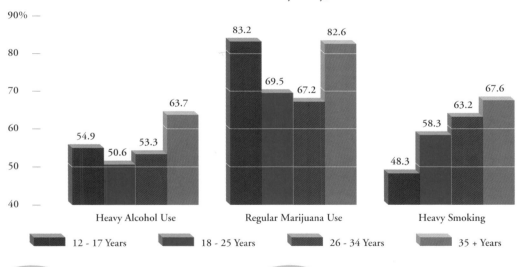

Heavy Alcohol Use: 54.9, 50.6, 53.3, 63.7
Regular Marijuana Use: 83.2, 69.5, 67.2, 82.6
Heavy Smoking: 48.3, 58.3, 63.2, 67.6

■ 12 - 17 Years   ■ 18 - 25 Years   ■ 26 - 34 Years   ■ 35 + Years

NOTES · · · · · · · · · · · · · · · · **SOURCES** ·

1a. *Data are percentages of high school seniors who see "great risk" of harm from smoking marijuana regularly; taking cocaine regularly; having five or more drinks once or twice each weekend; or smoking one or more* *packs of cigarettes per day.*
1b. *Heavy alcohol use is five or more drinks once or twice a week. Regular marijuana use is smoking marijuana regularly. Heavy smoking is smoking one or more packs per day.*

1a. *The University of Michigan News and Information Services, Press Release, April 9, 1993. Ann Arbor MI. Table 6.*
1b. *US Substance Abuse and Mental Health Services Administration,* *Office of Applied Studies.* National Household Survey on Drug Abuse: Highlights 1991. *Rockville MD. DHHS Pub. No. (SMA) 93-1979, 1993. Table A-25, p. 93.*

IMPLICATIONS OF EARLY USE

AGE IS ONE of the most important factors defining the likelihood of using alcohol, illicit drugs and tobacco. It also is related to subsequent patterns of use and problems associated with use. Young adults—people ages 18 to 25—are the group mostly likely to use alcohol or illicit drugs or engage in heavy alcohol use (Indicator 2). People ages 18 to 34 are the group most likely to smoke.

Many young people begin to experiment with alcohol, illicit drugs and tobacco at very early ages, although not all who try drugs once or twice continue to use them. By the 8th grade, 70 percent of youth report having tried alcohol, 10 percent have tried marijuana and 2 percent cocaine, and 44 percent have smoked cigarettes. By the 12th grade, about 88 percent have used alcohol, 37 percent have used marijuana and 8 percent cocaine, and 63 percent have smoked cigarettes. Clearly, substance use begins early for many young people. (Indicators 3 and 4).

Because cigarettes and alcohol usually are tried before illicit drugs such as marijuana, hallucinogens or cocaine, they often are referred to as "gateway drugs." However, many youth who use alcohol or cigarettes never try illegal drugs. The age when young people first start using alcohol and illicit drugs is a powerful predictor of later alcohol and drug problems, especially if use begins before age 15. People who begin using alcohol or smoking when very young are more likely to be heavy users of these substances later on.

Problems related to alcohol and drug dependence typically begin to be apparent by age 20. This is an important time for young people, as they complete school, enter the work force and begin to get married and have families. For women, problems with alcohol frequently occur later—when they are in their thirties.

3. Alcohol, Marijuana, and Cigarette Use Among Eighth Graders, 1991-1992

SOURCES

The University of Michigan News and Information Service, Press Release, April 9, 1993. Ann Arbor, MI. Table 1.

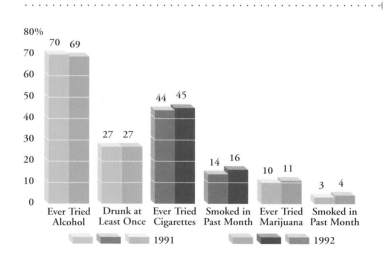

2. Prevalence of Substance Use, 1991

Percent of Users in Past Month

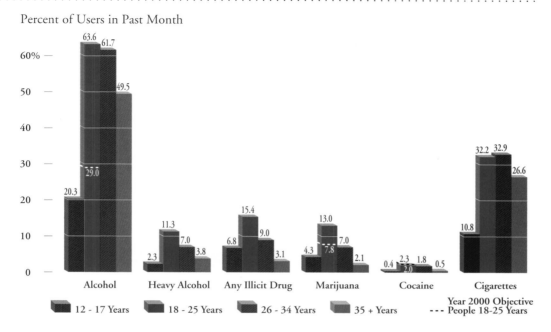

| | 12 - 17 Years | | 18 - 25 Years | | 26 - 34 Years | | 35 + Years | Year 2000 Objective
- - - People 18-25 Years |

4. Early Experimentation, 1991

Average Age of First Use

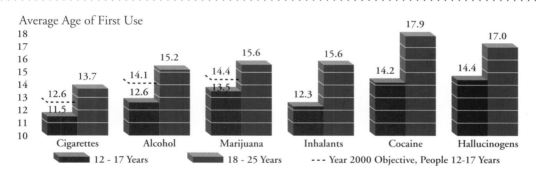

| | 12 - 17 Years | | 18 - 25 Years | - - - Year 2000 Objective, People 12-17 Years |

SOURCES

2. US National Institute on Drug Abuse. National Household Survey on Drug Abuse: Population Estimates 1991. *Rockville, MD. DHHS Pub. No. (ADM) 92-1887, 1992. Table 2-A, p. 19, Table 3-A, p. 25, Table 4-A, p. 31, Table 13-A, p. 85, and Table 14-A, p. 91.*

US Substance Abuse and Mental Health Services Administration, Office of Applied Studies. National Household Survey on Drug Abuse: Highlights 1991. *Rockville, MD. DHHS Pub. No. (SMA)93-1979, 1993. Table A-22, p. 90.*
4. US Substance Abuse and Mental

Health Services Adminstration, Office of Applied Studies. National Household Survey on Drug Abuse: Main findings 1991. *Rockville, MD. DHHS Pub. No. (SMA) 93-1980, 1993. Table 10.5, p. 137.*

TRENDS IN HEAVY USE

AT FIRST GLANCE, the statistics look promising: The overall use of cigarettes, alcohol and illicit drugs among most segments of the population has declined in recent years. However, the number of heavy, frequent users has remained more stable. Heavy smoking is often defined as smoking a pack or more of cigarettes per day; heavy drinking usually means consuming five or more drinks per occasion on five or more days in the past 30 days; and heavy drug use may be considered to be daily or weekly use.

To indicate how much heavy drinkers actually consume, half of the alcohol consumed in this country is accounted for by the 10 percent of the population who drink the most heavily. Heavy drinking has decreased in recent years, from 6.5 percent of the population age 12 and older in 1985 to 5.3 percent in 1991 (table). Nevertheless, heavy drinking among high school seniors and college students is still of concern and is one of the *Healthy People 2000* targets for reduction.

The decrease in people using illicit drugs since the late 1970s has been even more dramatic. At that time, almost 40 percent of high school seniors were using drugs. In 1992, in contrast, 14 percent of the senior class reported using drugs. For people ages 18 to 25—the age group with the highest rates of illicit drug use—marijuana use peaked at 35 percent in 1979 and fell to 13 percent in 1991. Cocaine use among this age group also peaked in 1979 at nine percent and dropped to two percent in 1991.

Between 1985 and 1991, the number of people who reported being frequent cocaine users (once a week or more) also decreased, but the decline was not statistically significant (Indicator 5). Heavy drug use is a particularly difficult problem in many urban areas, where hard core users become concentrated and drug-related crime flourishes.

Cigarette use also has decreased over the past decades — specifically since the 1964 publication of the Surgeon General's report on the health effects of smoking. The proportion of the adult population who smoked decreased from 42 percent in 1965 to 26 percent in 1991. Despite this overall decline in smokers, the proportion of heavy smokers—those who smoke 25 or more cigarettes a day—has not changed much. In 1991, 15 percent of the population, or 56 percent of smokers, smoked a pack or more per day.

TABLE · SOURCES · · · · · · · · ·

TRENDS IN ALCOHOL USE, U.S. HOUSEHOLD POPULATION

	1985	1988	1990	1991
Any alcohol use in past month	59.1%	53.4%	59.2%	50.9%
Heavy alcohol use in past month	6.5	4.9	5.0	5.3

US National Institute on Drug Abuse. National Household Survey on Drug Abuse, 1985-1991.

5. Trends in Cocaine Use

Number of Users

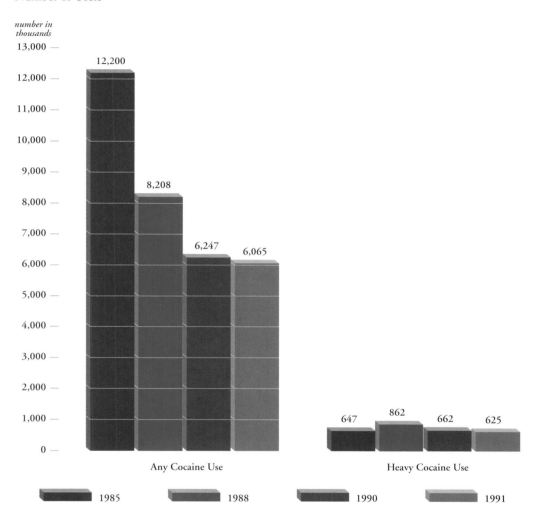

number in thousands

Any Cocaine Use

Heavy Cocaine Use

12,200 — 1985
8,208 — 1988
6,247
6,065

647 862 662 625

1985   1988   1990   1991

NOTES

Any cocaine use is at least once in the past year. Heavy cocaine use is once a week or more in the past year.

SOURCES

Gfroerer JC and Brodsky MD. Frequent Cocaine Users and Their Use of Treatment. American Journal of Public Health, *Vol. 83, No. 8, Fig. 1, p 1150, 1993. US National Institute on*

Drug Abuse. National Household Survey on Drug Abuse: Population Estimates 1990. *Rockville, MD. DHHS Pub. No. (ADM) 91-1732, 1991. Table 20-A, p. 111.*

DEMOGRAPHIC DIFFERENCES IN HEAVY USE

DIFFERENT POPULATION GROUPS differ in their rates of heavy use of tobacco, alcohol, and illicit drugs. These variations are most apparent by race and ethnicity, gender, and education.

White high school seniors are most likely and blacks least likely to be heavy smokers and drinkers; Hispanics fall in between (Indicator 6). Blacks have met the *Healthy People 2000* objective for a reduction of heavy drinking.

Although heavy smoking and drinking have decreased among all racial and ethnic groups, the decreases in heavy smoking among black youth have been particularly dramatic. Blacks have continued to decrease their smoking while the rates of other groups have stabilized. Among racial and ethnic groups, young Native American males tend to be heavier smokers and drinkers. Recent studies show that about 48 percent of male Native American and white high school seniors drank heavily, compared with 45 percent of Mexican-Americans, 24 percent of blacks, and 19 percent of Asian-Americans; some 18 percent of male Native American high school seniors smoked 1/2 pack or more a day, compared with 12 percent of whites, five percent of Mexican-Americans,

and 4 percent of Asian-Americans.

There also are differences in substance use by gender, but these patterns are in flux. Since the mid-1970s, male high school seniors have been more likely than females to use marijuana or alcohol daily, but now the gap between the sexes is narrowing. Meanwhile, for most of this period, female high school seniors have been more likely than males to smoke daily, but trends are changing here, too, and now more high school males smoke daily than females.

Among people of all ages, males are more than three times as likely as females to be heavy drinkers and somewhat more likely to smoke a pack or more of cigarettes per day. Males also are more than twice as likely as females to use marijuana once a week or more, but males and females are equally likely to be weekly cocaine users.

Where people live and their educational level also relate to substance use. Heavy alcohol use is more common among people living in metropolitan areas and among those with less than a college degree. Heavy smokers are more likely to live in nonmetropolitan areas and to be less educated—having a high school diploma or less.

6. Heavy Alcohol and Daily Cigarette Use Among Young People

Percent of High School Seniors Who are Heavy Users

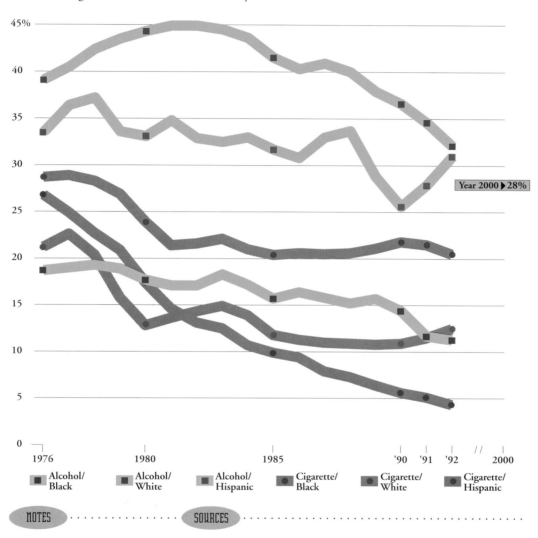

Year 2000 ▶ 28%

Alcohol/Black Alcohol/White Alcohol/Hispanic Cigarette/Black Cigarette/White Cigarette/Hispanic

NOTES · **SOURCES** ·

Each point plotted is the mean of the specified year and the previous year. "Hispanic" is derived from self-report. "Heavy alcohol use" is five or more drinks in a row in the past two weeks.

US National Institute on Drug Abuse. Smoking, Drinking, and Illicit Drug Use Among American Secondary School Students, College Students, and Young Adults, 1975-1991. Volume I: Sec-

ondary School Students. Rockville, MD. NIH Pub. No. 93-3480, 1992. Figure 17b, p.111. Unpublished data from the US National Institute on Drug Abuse, High School Senior Survey, 1992.

ATTEMPTS TO QUIT

MANY PEOPLE WHO smoke, drink or use drugs have experienced some kind of problem related to use and have tried to stop. Because quitting use of any of these substances is hard, the relapse rate is high, and some people have to try numerous times before they are successful.

Depending on personal characteristics and the substance being used, some users become dependent or need larger amounts to achieve the same effect. Other symptoms of dependence are daily use for two or more weeks, feeling a need for the substance, trying to cut down and withdrawal symptoms. One-third of people who used alcohol, marijuana, or cocaine experienced one or more of these symptoms. In fact, cigarettes are most likely to induce dependence, and 82 percent of those who smoked in the past year report having these symptoms.

To break the smoking habit, many people try to quit or cut back on their own. The typical smoker who becomes a confirmed former smoker usually has tried three or four times before being successful.

More than 44 million Americans have quit smoking, and almost half of all living adults in the United States who ever smoked have quit. The percentage of smokers who quit increased dramatically after the release of the 1964 Surgeon General's report that documented the negative health effects of smoking (Indicator 7). The percent of people who ever smoked who now are former smokers is higher among the elderly than other age groups, among men than women, among whites than blacks and among college graduates than those with less education. Despite the increase in the percentage who have quit, about 46 million Americans still smoke cigarettes.

TABLE · **SOURCES** · · · · · · · · · · · · · · ·

CIGARETTE SMOKING QUITTING CONTINUUM

	Percent of People 20+ Who Have Ever Smoked, 1987
1. Current smokers who had never tried to quit	*19%*
2. Current smokers who had tried to quit but not in past year	*20*
3. Current smokers who had quit for 1-6 days in past year	*7*
4. Current smokers who had quit for 7 or more days in past year	*8*
5. Former smokers who had quit within past 3 months	*2*
6 Former smokers who had been abstinent for 3-12 months	*3*
7. Former smokers who had been abstinent for 1-5 years	*10*
8. Former smokers who had quit more than 5 years earlier	*31*

US Centers for Disease Control. The Health Benefits of Smoking Cessation. *Rockville, MD. DHHS Pub. No. (CDC) 90-8416, 1990. Table 2, p. 589.*

7. Smokers Who Have Quit

Percent of People 20+ Who Ever Smoked Who Now Have Quit

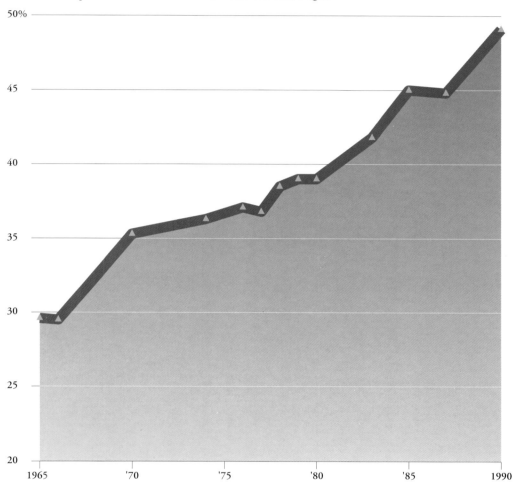

SOURCES

1965-1987 data: US Centers for Disease Control. The Health Benefits of Smoking Cessation. *Rockville, MD. DHHS Pub. No. (CDC) 90-S416, 1990.*

Table 3, p. 592. 1990 data: US Centers for Disease Control. Morbidity and Mortality Weekly Report, Cigarette Smoking Among Adults, US 1990. *Volume 41, No. 20. Atlanta, GA. May, 1992. p. 355*

FURTHER READING

PERCEPTION OF RISK

Bachman, JG, Johnston, LD, O'Malley, P, Humphrey, RN. "Explaining the Recent Decline in Marijuana Use: Differentiating the Effects of Perceived Risks, Disapproval, and General Lifestyle Factors." *Journal of Health and Social Behavior,* 29 (March): 92-112, 1988.

IMPLICATIONS OF EARLY USE

Christie, KA, Burke, JD, Regier, DA, Rae, DS, Boyd, JH, Locke, BZ. "Epidemiologic Evidence for Early Onset of Mental Disorders and Higher Risk of Drug Abuse in Young Adults." *American Journal of Psychiatry,* 145: 971-975, 1988.

TRENDS IN HEAVY USE

Gfroerer, JC, Brodsky, MD. "Frequent Cocaine Users and Their Use of Treatment." *American Journal of Public Health,* 83(8): 1149-1154, 1993.

DEMOGRAPHIC DIFFERENCES IN HEAVY USE

Bachman, JG, Wallace, JM, O'Malley, PM, Johnston, LD, Kurth, CL, Neighbors, HW. "Racial/Ethnic Differences In Smoking, Drinking and Illicit Drug Use Among American High School Seniors, 1976-1989." *American Journal of Public Health,* 81(3): 372-377, 1991.

ATTEMPTS TO QUIT

U.S. Centers for Disease Control. *The Health Benefits of Smoking Cessation.* Rockville, MD.: DHHS Pub. No. (CDC) 90-S416, 1990.

Schelling, TC. "Addictive Drugs: The Cigarette Experience." *Science,* 255: 430-433, 1992.

▸*Each year, nearly half a million Americans die from alcohol, tobacco, and illicit drugs, making substance abuse the single largest preventable cause of death in the country.*

▸*A person dying from alcohol-related causes loses, on average, 26 years off the normal life span; drug-related causes, over 37 years; and smoking-related causes, about 20 years.*

▸*AIDS among injecting drug users is the fastest growing cause of death among substance abusers.*

▸*Substance abuse drives up health care costs. Between 25 and 40 percent of all general hospital patients are there because of complications related to alcoholism.*

▸*Nearly one adult in five lived with an alcoholic or problem drinker as a child.*

▸*At least half of all people arrested for major crimes—including homicide, theft, and assault—were using illicit drugs at the time of their arrest.*

TOBACCO DEATHS

CIGARETTE SMOKING ACCOUNTS for nearly 419,000 deaths a year—20 percent of all U.S. deaths (Indicator 8a). More than 3.6 million years of life would have been saved if every person who died in just one year from cigarette smoking had lived until average life expectancy. Nearly all deaths associated with smoking result from a smoking habit acquired early in life.

Cigarette smoking has long been known to cause cancer, and nearly 90 percent of lung cancer deaths result from smoking. Lung cancer rates, always high among men, have risen among both men and women in the last few decades (Indicator 8b). Lung cancer deaths now surpass deaths from all other kinds of cancer—exceeding prostate cancer in men and breast cancer in women.

While lung cancer rates are a good marker for long-term use of tobacco, lung cancer accounts for only one-quarter of all deaths attributed to smoking. Smoking also is a major contributor in deaths from coronary heart disease, chronic bronchitis and emphysema, and cancers of the pancreas, trachea, bronchus, and larynx. Further, smoking during pregnancy is associated with fetal and infant deaths. In fact, smoking is probably the most important modifiable cause of poor pregnancy outcome, according to the U.S. Surgeon General.

Most deaths associated with smoking occur among the smokers themselves, but exposure to environmental tobacco smoke also is an acknowledged health hazard and each year results in about 3,000 deaths among nonsmokers from cancer and other causes. Many people are exposed to tobacco smoke in the workplace, as well as at home from family members who smoke, and more than half of nonsmokers working in companies with minimal smoking restrictions say others' smoking causes them at least some discomfort. With the increase in smoke-free workplaces, second-hand smoke exposure—at least at work—is likely to decline.

8a. Deaths from Smoking and Alcohol Use: Total

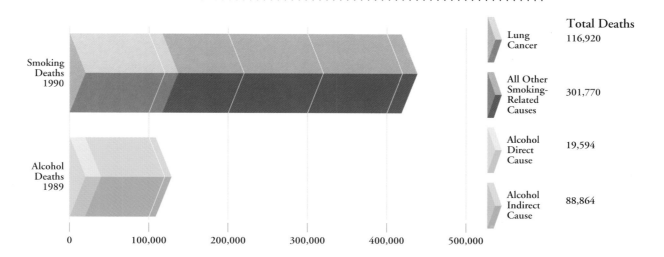

	Total Deaths
Lung Cancer	116,920
All Other Smoking-Related Causes	301,770
Alcohol Direct Cause	19,594
Alcohol Indirect Cause	88,864

8b. Deaths from Lung Cancer

Age-Adjusted Lung Cancer Deaths Per 100,000 People

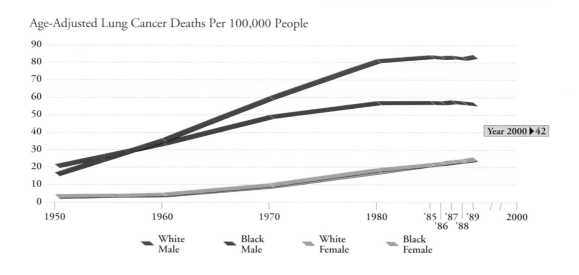

Year 2000 ▶ 42

White Male   Black Male   White Female   Black Female

NOTES

Lung cancers and other smoking deaths are estimates of deaths where smoking is an attributable factor, including cardiovascular and cerebrovascular diseases.
8b. Analysis of National Vital Statistics System. Lung cancer refers to all respiratory cancers.

SOURCES

8a. *Smoking: US Office on Smoking and Health. 1990 SAMMEC Mortality Estimates.* Morbidity and Mortality Weekly Report, *forthcoming.*
Alcohol: Stinson FS, Dufour MC, Steffens R, and DeBakey SF. Epidemiologic Bulletin 32: Alcohol-Related Mortal-

ity, 1979-1989. Alcohol Health and Research World, *forthcoming.*
8b. *US National Center for Health Statistics.* Health, United States, 1991 and Prevention Profile. *Hyattsville, MD: DHHS Pub. No. (PHS)92-1232, 1992. Table 36, p. 169-170.*

ALCOHOL DEATHS

LCOHOL IS A major cause of premature death in the United States (Indicator 8c). On average, people dying from alcohol-related causes lose 26 years from their normal life expectancy. The ninth leading cause of death—liver disease—is largely preventable, because nearly half of all cirrhosis deaths are due to alcohol.

Cirrhosis deaths are a marker of long-term alcohol use and accordingly are more prevalent among people in middle age and older. Since 1974, death rates for alcohol-related liver cirrhosis dropped 26 percent. This trend reflects the overall decline in alcohol consumption as well as an increase in the number of people recovering from heavy drinking because of treatment, health education programs, and other interventions.

Alcohol-related motor vehicle fatalities also continue to decline (Indicator 8d), and the death rate is now lower than the public health objective stated in *Healthy People 2000*. Between 1990 and 1991, the number of alcohol-related traffic fatalities dropped 10 percent, with the greatest decrease among young drivers ages 15 to 20. Still, traffic crashes remain the single greatest cause of death among America's youth and young adults, and almost half of all traffic fatalities are alcohol-related.

The recent decline in alcohol-related traffic fatalities may be due to declines in both chronic use and inappropriate use among even casual drinkers, particularly young people. Federal requirements to restrict access to alcohol for those under age 21 and legislation in some states to lower the allowable blood alcohol concentration for young people may in part explain the decline. Diverse efforts under way in communities across the country—including prompt license suspension, sobriety police checks, zero tolerance for underage drivers, and public education—such as "designated driver" programs—also may have had an impact on alcohol-impaired driving.

Evidence links drinking and deaths from falls, fires and burns, and drowning. Falls are the second leading cause of fatal injuries, and fires and burns are the fourth leading cause. Various studies estimate that between 17 and 53 percent of falls are alcohol-related, and between 48 and 64 percent of people dying in fires had blood alcohol levels indicating intoxication. One common cause of fire among intoxicated people is falling asleep or passing out with a lit cigarette.

8c. Deaths from Alcohol Use Over Time

Age-Adjusted Alcohol-Related Deaths Per 100,000 People

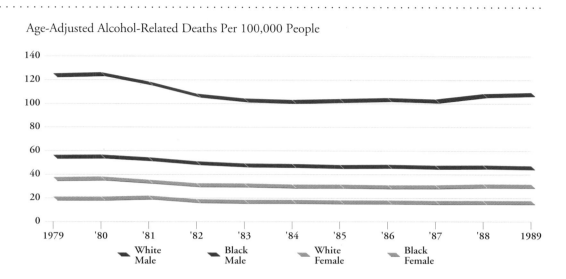

White Male · Black Male · White Female · Black Female

8d. Deaths from Alcohol-Related Traffic Injuries

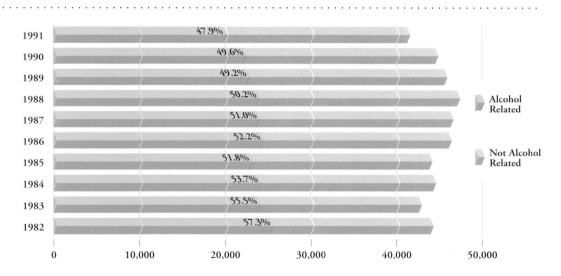

Alcohol Related

Not Alcohol Related

NOTES

8d. *Traffic fatalities are number of deaths from crashes in which at least one person dies within 30 days of the crash. National Highway Traffic Safety Administration* *defines a fatality or fatal crash as alcohol-related if either a driver or a nonmotorist (usually a pedestrian) had a blood alcohol concentration of 0.01% or above.*

SOURCES

8c. *Stinson FS, Dufour MC, Steffens R, and DeBakey SF. Epidemiologic Bulletin 32: Alcohol-Related Mortality, 1979-1989.* Alcohol Health and Research World, *forthcoming.*

8d. *US Department of Transportation, National Highway Traffic Safety Administration.* FARS Fatal Accident Reporting System, Annual Report, 1992 *forthcoming.*

ILLICIT DRUG DEATHS

DRUG-RELATED DEATHS are increasing—particularly among men, and even more so among black men. The number of people dying from conditions directly identified with illicit drugs in vital statistics reports (e.g., overdose) is more than one-half the number of deaths from conditions directly identified with alcohol. These drug deaths are rising (Indicator 8e). Adding in AIDS deaths among injecting drug users substantially increases the number.

Reported deaths directly related to drugs are gross underestimates of the mortality toll from illicit drugs since they exclude deaths from associated diseases, such as hepatitis or TB, and all other causes where illicit drugs contributed to death, such as homicides, falls and motor vehicle crashes. Medical examiner data from 1990 indicate that about one-third of all drug deaths involve illicit drugs as a contributing factor, but not the direct cause of death. Deaths from drug causes often involve a lethal combination of two or more illicit drugs or drugs combined with alcohol. Heroin or cocaine is involved in two-thirds of drug deaths.

Nearly 40 percent of illicit drug deaths are among adults between 30 and 39 years old, an age group that has high rates of many chronic problems due to drug abuse. Overall, rates are higher for men than for women, and for blacks than for whites (Indicator 8f). Black men are more than twice as likely as white men to die from the direct effects of illicit drugs, and black women are nearly twice as likely as white women to die from drug use. Between 1979 and 1989, the rate for black men rose 133 percent, compared to a 50 percent increase for white men and black women, while rates among white women actually dropped. Only the rate for white women falls below that targeted by *Healthy People 2000*.

The fastest growing cause of all illicit drug-related deaths is AIDS. More than 33 percent of new AIDS cases occur among injecting drug users or people having sexual contact with them. In 1984—the first year AIDS deaths were tallied reliably—989 AIDS deaths occurred among injecting drug users and their sexual partners. By 1989, these two groups accounted for 7,700 AIDS deaths.

Even non-users can be victims of a drug-related death—for example, people killed in drug-related violence or motor vehicle crashes related to illicit drug use, or the sexual partners of HIV-infected drug users. The number of these deaths is not fully known, but clearly a significant cost imposed upon American society by illicit drug abuse.

8e. Alcohol and Illicit Drug Deaths Over Time

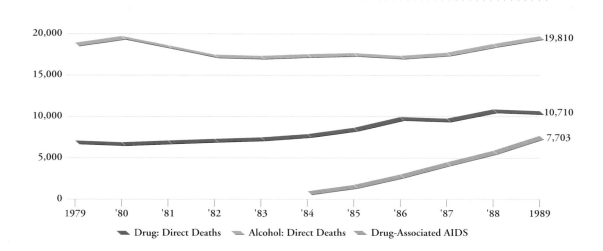

19,810

10,710

7,703

➤ Drug: Direct Deaths   ➤ Alcohol: Direct Deaths   ➤ Drug-Associated AIDS

8f. Deaths Directly Caused by Illicit Drugs

Age-Adjusted Deaths Per 100,000 People

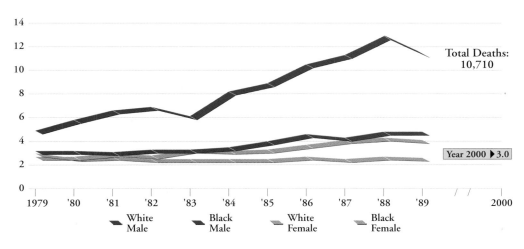

Total Deaths: 10,710

Year 2000 ▶ 3.0

➤ White Male   ➤ Black Male   ➤ White Female   ➤ Black Female

NOTES

8e. *Alcohol-direct and drug-direct deaths are conservative because they exclude accidents, homicides, and other causes related to alcohol or illicit drug use but not directly caused by them.*

SOURCES

8e. *Alcohol and Drugs: US National Center for Health Statistics.* Advance Report of Final Mortality Statistics, 1989. *Monthly Vital Statistics Report, Vol. 40, No. 8, Supplement 2, 1992.*

AIDS: US National Center for Health Statistics. Health, United States, 1991 and Prevention Profile, *1992 .* 8f. *US National Center for Health Statistics. See 8e, first citation.*

WHEN USED FOR long periods of time, tobacco, alcohol and illicit drugs can impair most major organ systems. As examples, tobacco and alcohol use are major risk factors for diseases of the heart and blood vessels; and tobacco use also leads to chronic bronchitis and emphysema, cancers and infections, and pregnancy complications. Other risky behaviors associated with alcohol and illicit drug use increase the risk of acquiring the human immunodeficiency virus (HIV). Using these substances during pregnancy can lead to a lifetime of disability for the offspring.

Thus, substance abuse adds considerably to the nation's total health care bill. These costs are for treating a host of illnesses and injuries associated with smoking, drinking and using illicit drugs, and include services given in physician's offices, hospitals, emergency rooms and other treatment facilities.

In any given year, a smoker uses more medical care than a person who has never smoked, and when heavy smokers are hospitalized, they stay 25 percent longer than do nonsmokers. Likewise, problem drinkers average four times as many days in the hospital as nondrinkers, mostly because of drinking-related injuries. Studies show that as much as 40 percent of all patients in general hospitals are there because of complications related to alcoholism. Illicit drug users—particularly people using cocaine or heroin—make more than 370,000 visits to costly emergency rooms each year, and since both alcohol and drug use may result in serious injury, people using these substances disproportionately need care in high-cost trauma treatment centers.

Most of the health care costs attributed to alcohol and illicit drug abuse are for treatment in general or short-stay hospitals, including their intensive care units (ICUs) (Indicator 9). About 28 percent of all ICU admissions and nearly 40 percent of all ICU costs at one major hospital were attributed to substance abuse. People who smoked were more frequently admitted to the ICU than were alcohol or drug users and incurred higher ICU costs.

Specialized treatment centers also play their part in substance abusers' care. These include both residential and outpatient treatment centers. Care in specialty alcohol treatment centers costs more than $3 billion a year and in drug treatment centers nearly $900 million. Nursing homes deliver services for smokers and drinkers debilitated by chronic health problems, and more than 10 percent of all the medical costs associated with tobacco and alcohol come from nursing home care.

9. Direct Health Care Costs of Alcohol and Drug Abuse, 1990

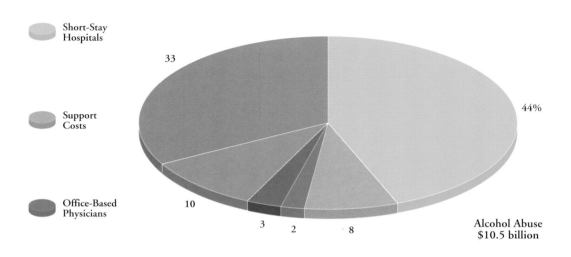

Short-Stay
Hospitals

Support
Costs

Office-Based
Physicians

Alcohol Abuse
$10.5 billion

Other Professional
Services

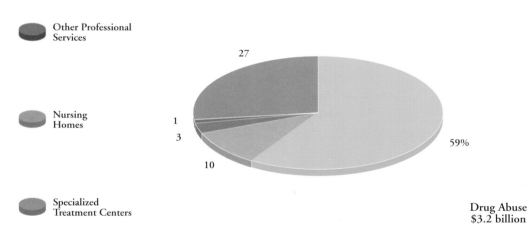

Nursing
Homes

Specialized
Treatment Centers

Drug Abuse
$3.2 billion

NOTES

These costs are based on socioeconomic indexes applied to 1985 estimates. Office-based physician costs include visits to psychiatrists. Other professional services include: psychologists, social workers, nurses, physical and occupational therapists, pharmacists, technologists, and others. Support costs related to alcohol and drugs include expenditures for research, training costs for doctors, nurses, and program administrators and private insurance for alcohol and drug disorders.

SOURCES

Unpublished data for 1990 from Dorothy P. Rice. Institute for Health and Aging, University of California at San Francisco, CA 94143-0612.

EFFECTS OF SUBSTANCE ABUSE ON FAMILIES

SUBSTANCE ABUSE PLACES tremendous psychological and financial burdens on families. Nearly 20 percent of men and more than 25 percent of women say that drinking has been a cause of trouble in their family. As high as these figures are, the prevalence of substance abuse and family problems is no doubt seriously under-reported (Indicator 10).

Problem drinking can affect a family in many ways, even causing its break-up. More than one-third of women who are separated or divorced were married at one time to a problem drinker or alcoholic. Families with problem drinkers experience a host of social problems, such as violence between spouses, child abuse and a higher likelihood of raising children—particularly boys— who themselves become problem drinkers. Almost one-fifth of adults say that they lived with a problem drinker or an alcoholic when they were children.

Children in alcoholic families exhibit emotional and adjustment difficulties. These problems include aggressive behavior, difficulties with peers, conduct problems, bouts of hyperactivity and poor school adjustment. In addition, these youngsters miss school more often and have more physical ailments and serious injuries than do children raised in non-alcoholic homes. Children whose parents smoke also have more health problems associated with tobacco smoke, such as respiratory infections and decreased pulmonary function and lung growth.

Reports of child neglect and abuse have increased rapidly in recent years, and many such incidents are believed to be directly related to illicit drug—and possibly alcohol—use among parents. In New York, crack is blamed for the threefold increase in the city's child abuse and neglect cases in the late 1980s.

Another impact of substance use on families is the financial drain. The costs of smoking and drinking can be high (Indicator 11). These costs are calculated for all households, not just those with smokers and drinkers; $800 to $900 a year could be spent on four six-packs of beer a week, and a two-pack-a-day smoker could spend over $1,300 a year on cigarettes. If the impact of cocaine use and other illicit drugs were calculated, its effects on a family budget would be staggering.

10. People with Alcoholics or Problem Drinkers in the Family, 1988

Percent of Adults

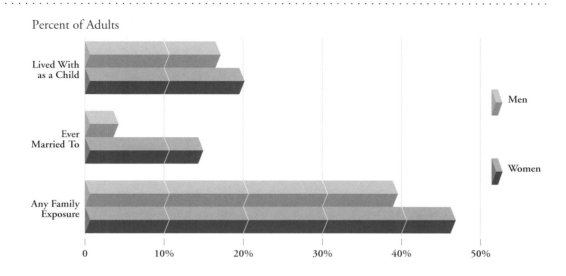

11. Annual Household Expenses for Alcohol and Tobacco, 1991

Average Per Family

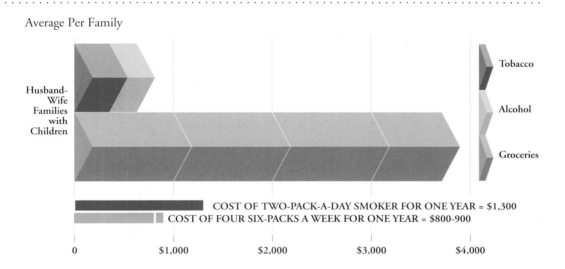

COST OF TWO-PACK-A-DAY SMOKER FOR ONE YEAR = $1,300
COST OF FOUR SIX-PACKS A WEEK FOR ONE YEAR = $800-900

SOURCES

10. *Schoenborn CA.* Exposure to Alcoholism in the Family. *Advance data from vital and health statistics, National Center for Health Statistics; No. 205, September 30, 1991. Table 1,* p.9, Table 2, p.10, and Table 4, p.12.

11. *US Department of Labor, Bureau of Labor Statistics.* Consumer Expenditures in 1991. *Washington, DC: USGPO 342-555/ 76921, 1992.*

RELATIONSHIP TO CRIME

THE LINK BETWEEN alcohol or illicit drug use and crime is visible every day in courtrooms, jails, and prisons across the country. Many offenders were under the influence of drugs, or alcohol, or both when they committed their crime. Others illegally sold them. In 1990, more than 1 million arrests were made for drug offenses (sales/manufacturing and possession) and more than 3 million for alcohol offenses (driving under the influence, liquor law violations, drunkenness, and disorderly conduct).

Illicit drugs and alcohol are partners in many violent crimes as well. At least half of the people arrested for major crimes such as homicide, theft, and assault were using illicit drugs around the time of their arrest (Indicator 12), and about half the people in state prisons for committing violent crimes report they were under the influence of alcohol or drugs at the time of their offense.

Alcohol is more likely to be involved in crimes against people than property. In about one-half to two-thirds of homicides and serious assaults, alcohol is present in either the offender, the victim, or both.

Women make up a small proportion of inmates (9 percent in jails and 4 percent in state prisons), but illicit drugs figure importantly in their incarceration. Among convicted jail inmates in 1989, for example, females were more likely than males to have ever used these drugs (84 percent vs. 77 percent), to have used them daily in the month before their current offense (40 percent vs. 29 percent), and to have been under their influence at the time of the offense (31 percent vs. 17 percent). In contrast, males were about twice as likely as females to have been under the influence of alcohol at the time of their offense (44 percent vs. 21 percent).

12. Arrestees Testing Positive for Illicit Drugs, 1991

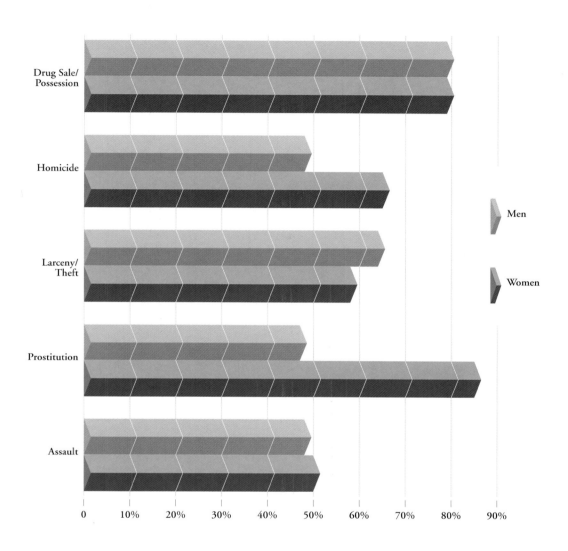

NOTES

Testing using urinalysis is done for cocaine, opiates, marijuana, PCP, methadone, benzodiazepines, methaqualone, propoxyphene, barbiturates, and amphetamines. Data are collected in 24 cities on persons arrested during a specific two-week time period.

SOURCES

US Department of Justice, National Institute of Justice. 1991 Drug Use Forecasting Annual Report. *Washington, DC: NCJ-136045, 1993. p. 21.*

WORKPLACE BURDEN

A SIGNIFICANT AMOUNT OF substance use takes place among the American work force, and some of this use occurs at work. One-third of full-time workers are smokers, about two-thirds report that they consumed alcohol in the past month, and about 15 percent say they used illicit drugs during the past year.

Smoking is a costly burden for employers. In addition to health care costs for the smokers, smoking poses health hazards to non-smokers at work and increases the risk of workplace fires and product contamination, as well as the cost of facility cleaning and ventilation. Each year employers may pay thousands of dollars per smoker to cover these costs.

Smoking is most common among workers who earn less than $10,000 a year. The more people earn, the less likely they are to smoke. Smoking also is more common among certain occupations, including handlers/cleaners, protective service workers, transportation/material movers and machinists, and it is more hazardous in certain chemical industries where tobacco smoke can interact with occupational exposures and exacerbate health risks.

Illicit drug and alcohol use also are costly to employers. Health insurance costs for employees with alcohol problems are about twice those of other employees. In addition, there are the costs of related workplace injuries—including those in company-owned vehicles—higher employee turnover and lost productivity. Two-thirds of drug users work full or part-time (chartlet). Some 27 percent of full-time employed illicit drug users report that in the past 30 days they had missed work due to illness or injury, and 18 percent had simply skipped work (Indicator 13).

Fifteen percent of illicit drug users and 6 percent of heavy alcohol users say they had actually gone to work high or a little drunk in the past year. During the year before employees begin drug or alcohol treatment, two out of five report that they worked under the influence at least once a week.

Since evidence shows that treatment can reduce job-related problems and result in abstinence, many employers sponsor employee assistance programs (EAPs), conduct drug-testing, or have policies or procedures to detect substance use and promote early treatment. Nationally, at least 30 percent of employees have access to an EAP, and 20 percent work in firms with a drug testing program. Workplace smoking cessation programs are increasingly popular as well.

EMPLOYMENT
STATUS OF ILLICIT
DRUG USERS, 1991

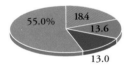

55.0% 18.4 13.6 13.0

- ■ Employed Full-Time
- ■ Employed Part-Time
- ■ Unemployed
- ■ Other

Notes:
▲ *"Other" includes people who are retired, disabled, homemakers, and students.*

Sources:
▲ *US National Institute on Drug Abuse.* National Household Survey on Drug Abuse. *Press Release, December 19, 1991.*

13. Alcohol and Drug Users Have Problems Working, 1991

Full-Time Employees with Problems

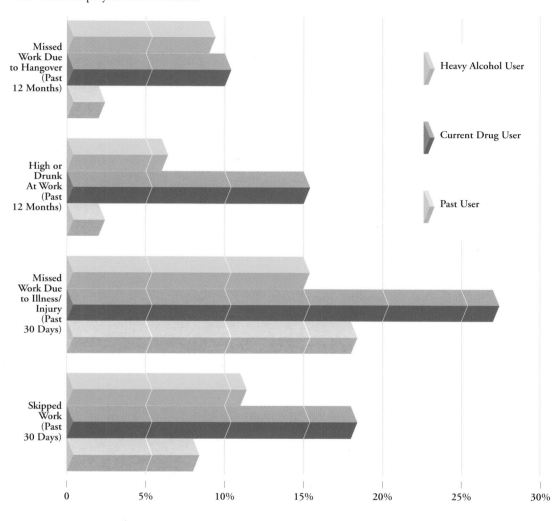

Legend:
- Heavy Alcohol User
- Current Drug User
- Past User

Categories (y-axis):
- Missed Work Due to Hangover (Past 12 Months)
- High or Drunk At Work (Past 12 Months)
- Missed Work Due to Illness/Injury (Past 30 Days)
- Skipped Work (Past 30 Days)

X-axis: 0, 5%, 10%, 15%, 20%, 25%, 30%

NOTES

Heavy alcohol users are people who drank five or more drinks per occasion on five or more days in the past 30 days. Current drug users are people who used any illicit drugs in the past month. Past users are those who used an illicit drug or alcohol in the past, but who are not current drug or heavy alcohol users.

SOURCES

Unpublished data from the 1991 National Household Survey on Drug Abuse. US Substance Abuse and Mental Health Services Administration, Office of Applied Studies.

FURTHER READING

TOBACCO DEATHS

U.S. Centers for Disease Control. *Reducing the Health Consequences of Smoking: 25 Years of Progress.* Rockville, MD: DHHS Pub. No. (CDC) 89-8411, 1989.

ALCOHOL DEATHS

U.S. Centers for Disease Control. Alcohol-Related Mortality and Years of Potential Life Lost–United States, 1987. *Morbidity and Mortality Weekly Report* 39 (11): 173-177, 1990.

U.S. Centers for Disease Control. Factors Potentially Associated with Reductions in Alcohol-Related Traffic Fatalities—United States, 1990 and 1991. *Morbidity and Mortality Weekly Report* 41(48): 893-899, 1992.

ILLICIT DRUG DEATHS

U.S. National Institute on Drug Abuse. *Annual Medical Examiner Data 1990.* Data from the Drug Abuse Warning Network (DAWN) Statistical Series. Series 1, Number 10-B. Rockville, MD: US DHHS Pub. No. (ADM) 91-1840, 1991.

STRAINS ON THE NATION'S HEALTH CARE SYSTEM

Blose, JO, Holder, HD. Injury-Related Medical Care Utilization in a Problem-Drinking Population. *American Journal of Public Health,* 81 (12): 1571-1575, 1991.

Hodgson, TA. Cigarette Smoking and Lifetime Medical Expenditures. *The Milbank Quarterly* 70 (1): 81-125, 1992.

EFFECTS OF SUBSTANCE ABUSE ON FAMILIES

Bijur, PE, Kerzon, M, Overpeck, MD, Scheidt, PC. Parental Alcohol Use, Problem Drinking, and Children's Injuries. *Journal of the American Medical Association* 267 (23): 3166-3171, 1992.

Schoenborn, CA. Exposure to Alcoholism in the Family: United States, 1988. *Advance Data from Vital and Health Statistics of the National Center for Health Statistics.* 205: September 30, 1991.

RELATIONSHIP TO CRIME

U.S. Bureau of Justice Statistics. *Drugs, Crime and the Justice System: A National Report from the Bureau of Justice Statistics.* Washington, DC: NCJ-133652, 1992.

WORKPLACE BURDEN

U.S. Bureau of Labor Statistics. *Survey of Employer Antidrug Programs.* Washington, DC: US Department of Labor, Bureau of Labor Statistics, Report 760, 1989.

Moore, KA. The High Cost of Smoking. *Business and Health Special Report: A Look at Smoking in the Workplace.* pp. 9-11, 1993.

▸ *The public is growing increasingly intolerant of substance use: 66 percent of Americans favor restricting public smoking, and nearly 90 percent favor automatic license suspension for first-time convictions for driving under the influence.*

▸ *Alcohol and cigarette excise taxes generate billions of dollars in government revenue and discourage consumption. A 50-cent increase in the cigarette tax will result in 2.5 million fewer smokers.*

▸ *More than 3 million arrests are made each year for alcohol-related offenses. The most common offense is driving under the influence.*

▸ *In 1989, 2.6 million underage youths smoked; half of them bought their own cigarettes.*

▸ *Arrests for drug violations are increasing, and the number of drug offenders in federal prisons grew from 5,000 in 1980 to 30,000 in 1991 and in state prisons from 17,500 in 1979 to 150,000 in 1991.*

▸ *About 5 million drug abusers and 18 million alcohol abusers need treatment, but only a fraction receive it.*

▸ *The majority of the 46 million American adults who currently smoke would like to quit.*

PUBLIC ATTITUDES

PUBLIC INTOLERANCE OF substance abuse is growing among Americans, and for more than a decade the public has looked more favorably on restricting the use of cigarettes, alcohol, and illicit drugs. This shift in attitudes is related in part to a rising awareness of the health impacts of substance abuse and to a greater health consciousness. Another factor is the association among alcohol, illicit drugs, and the nation's concern about crime.

Attitudes about smoking and drinking can vary depending on whether the use takes place in public or in private. In 1992, 54 percent of high school seniors thought getting drunk in public should be prohibited, while only 24 percent thought people should be prohibited from getting drunk in private (Indicator 14). About two-thirds of Americans favor restricting the use of cigarettes in various public places, including hotels, restaurants, and the workplace, and more than 40 percent support a total ban on smoking in public places.

The public also supports stringent sanctions against driving while intoxicated and, according to a national poll, would like to see tougher enforcement of drinking-age laws (64 percent), expanded use of police checkpoints to catch drunk drivers (79 percent), automatic license suspensions for the first offense (89 percent), and automatic confiscation of plates for the second offense (89 percent).

Attitudes about how to deal with illicit drug abuse are mixed. Some people see it as a law enforcement problem, which should be dealt with through arrests or border control. Others view it as a health problem, best handled through prevention, early intervention, and treatment. In response to a question about the most important government activity to address the drug problem, one public opinion poll found that 40 percent of Americans favored teaching young people about the dangers of drugs, while another 51 percent favored stopping the drug flow from other countries or arresting pushers or users. Another poll showed that 57 percent of the adult population favored using treatment programs to help drug users while 33 percent favored punishing them.

There is one area of agreement: For the last decade, the public has consistently thought that we spend too little on treatment. At least three-quarters of the public support using cigarette and alcohol taxes to pay for a bigger federal anti-drug program.

14. High School Seniors' Attitudes Toward Restrictions on Use

Percent Who Favor Prohibition of...

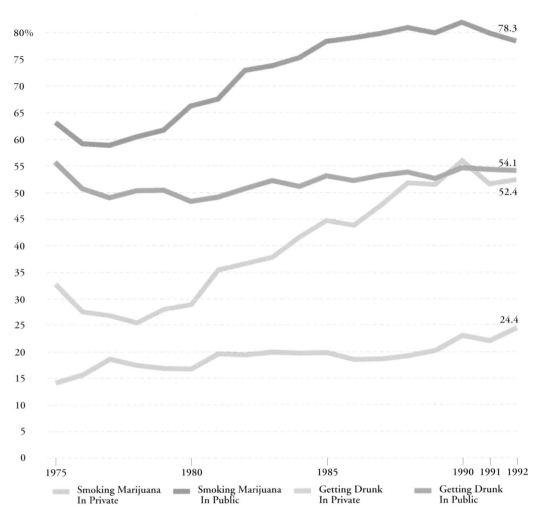

Smoking Marijuana In Private	Smoking Marijuana In Public	Getting Drunk In Private	Getting Drunk In Public

Values at right: 78.3, 54.1, 52.4, 24.4

X-axis: 1975, 1980, 1985, 1990 1991 1992

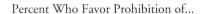

SOURCES

US National Institute on Drug Abuse. Drug Use Among American High School Seniors, College Students and Young Adults, 1975-1991. *Vol.1. NIH Pub. No. 93-3480, 1992. Table 23, p. 171.*

Unpublished data from the US National Institute on Drug Abuse High School Senior Survey, 1992.

ILLICIT DRUG CONTROL

THE TWO MAJOR strategies to control illegal drug use are: reducing the illicit drug supply and reducing Americans' demand for drugs. Supply-reduction strategies seek to curtail the supply of drugs through intercepting and seizing illegal drug shipments (interdiction), breaking up street market dealing, and other traditional law enforcement activities. Demand-reduction strategies aim to decrease the number of people who want to use illicit drugs, primarily through prevention, early intervention, and treatment services.

More money and effort traditionally have gone into supply reduction than demand reduction. Out of the total 1994 federal drug control budget of $13 billion, international and domestic law enforcement accounted for almost two-thirds, or $8.2 billion (Indicators 15a and 15b). The largest expenditures were for curtailing the imports of drugs (through interdiction, investigations and intelligence, and international efforts), followed by prosecution and corrections. Another major federal supply reduction activity is to intercept and seize drugs at the borders, and thwart use of air, land, and maritime routes for drug smuggling. Each year for the past several years, the U.S. Customs Service has made about 19,000 seizures with a retail value in excess of $12 billion. To achieve these seizures, the federal government has made major investments in interdiction equipment, including advanced communication and detection systems.

Despite spending $14 billion on interdiction over the last 10 years, the flow of illicit drugs into the United States has not slowed, and the worldwide production of cocaine, opium, and other drugs continues to increase. Intensified enforcement has not reduced the number of drug dealers or drug-related deaths and has had only limited success in raising drug prices.

State and local law enforcement agencies make more than 760,000 arrests for drug law violations a year. Of the total arrests in 1990, 68 percent were for possession and 32 percent for sales and manufacturing of illegal drugs. In recent years, the proportion of arrests has decreased for possession of drugs and increased for sales and manufacturing.

TABLE · **SOURCES** ·

DRUG OFFENDERS IN PRISON

	1979-80	1991
State Prisons	17,572	150,000
Federal Prisons	4,749	30,498

Federal data: The White House. National Drug Control Strategy. *Washington, DC: USGPO, 1992. State 1979 data: US Department of Justice.* Drugs, Crime, and the Justice System. *Washington, DC: NCJ-133652, 1992. State 1991 data: US Department of Justice.* Survey of State Prison Inmates, 1991. *Washington, DC: NCJ-136949, 1993.*

15a. Federal Drug Control Budget Over Time

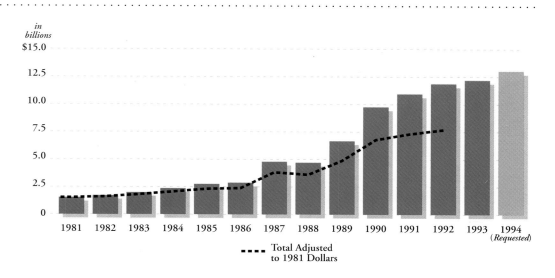

in billions

Total Adjusted to 1981 Dollars

1981 1982 1983 1984 1985 1986 1987 1988 1989 1990 1991 1992 1993 1994 *(Requested)*

15b. Federal Drug Control Budget Requested for 1994

Type of Activity

Prevention

Research & Development

International

Other Law Enforcement

Prosecution & Corrections

Interdiction

Investigations & Intelligence

Treatment

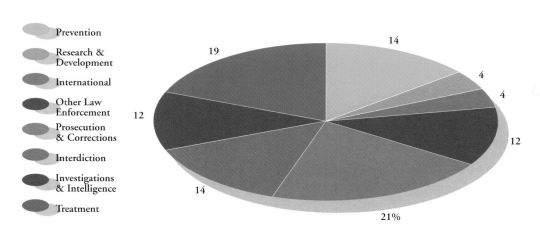

14

4

4

12

21%

14

12

19

SOURCES

15a. & 15b. *US Office of Management and Budget, Executive Office of the President.* Federal Drug Control Programs: Budget Summary Fiscal Year 1994. *Washington, DC: April 23, 1993, p.145-148.*

COMMUNITY COALITIONS

COMMUNITIES ACROSS THE country are responding to the impact of substance abuse in their neighborhoods by forming broad-based coalitions to fight back. The focus of most coalitions is on alcohol and illicit drugs, perhaps because the problems associated with them are so dramatic and obvious (Indicator 16). The federal Center for Substance Abuse Prevention has helped more than 250 communities set up "Partnerships" to reduce local problems from substance abuse. Coalitions exist in several thousand other communities, as well.

Much coalition activity focuses on prevention and early intervention for young people (table). Early intervention can reach people in the beginning stages of use and help them stop before serious problems develop. In some cases, intervention begins at the time of an arrest or in a youth detention facility. Early intervention programs—such as counseling, screening, and referrals to treatment— usually involve both the adolescent in trouble as well as the family. Prevention and early intervention activities include education on the consequences and risks of use and on giving people—particularly those at risk, such as chil-dren of substance abusers, the homeless, and school dropouts—the self-esteem and skills to avoid use.

Schools are involved in almost all of the community coalitions. In addition to educating students about the physical effects of substance use, schools can provide drug-free environments and activities that are alternatives to substance use. For example, many schools hold alcohol-free parties after proms and other school-sponsored events. Schools also have programs to educate parents about the pressures on their children to drink and use illicit drugs and how they can mitigate them. A consistent no-use message from parents helps young people avoid drugs and alcohol.

Other community work includes media campaigns such as those against drinking and driving sponsored by Students Against Driving Drunk (SADD) or the Partnership for a Drug-Free America's campaign depicting illicit drug use as risky to people, business, and the community. Messages such as "Friends don't let friends drive drunk" have become highly visible, and many beer companies have added a responsible drinking component to their advertising.

TABLE · SOURCES · · · · · · · · · · · ·

COMMUNITY COALITIONS REPORTING EXTENSIVE PROGRAM ACTIVITY, 1992

Prevention	*64%*
Early Intervention	*36*
Planning of System-wide Program	*33*
Impaired Driving Program	*32*
Treatment/Aftercare	*32*
Alcohol/Drug Related Health	*27*
Alcohol/Drug Related Crime	*26*

Join Together: A National Resource for Communities Fighting Substance Abuse. A National Study of Community-Based Anti-Drug and Alcohol Activity in America, *Boston, MA. 1992. Figure I, p. 8.*

16. Substances Targeted by Coalitions, 1992

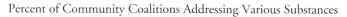

Percent of Community Coalitions Addressing Various Substances

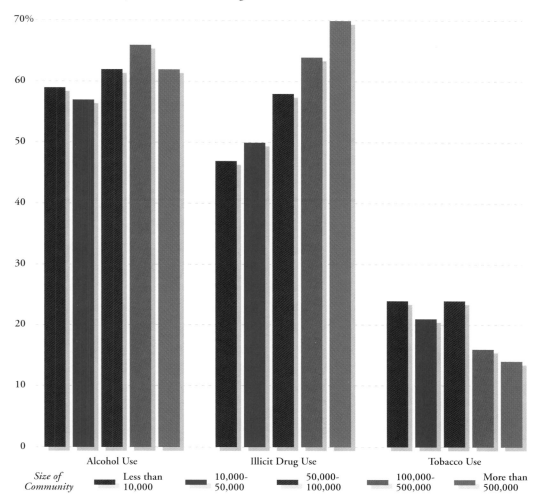

| Size of Community | Less than 10,000 | 10,000- 50,000 | 50,000- 100,000 | 100,000- 500,000 | More than 500,000 |

SOURCES

Join Together: A National Resource for Communities Fighting Substance Abuse. A National Study of Community-Based Anti-Drug and Alcohol Activity in America. *Boston, MA. 1992. Figure I, p. 8.*

ALCOHOL AND CIGARETTE TAXES

THE BILLIONS OF dollars collected each year in tobacco and alcohol taxes generate substantial revenue for government—and help pay for substance abuse prevention and treatment. These taxes also discourage consumption, especially among teenagers. Just one year after California raised its cigarette tax 25 cents in 1989—earmarking some of it for anti-smoking campaigns—per capita consumption declined 9 percent. Researchers estimate that a 50-cent tax increase would result in 2.5 million fewer smokers.

In fiscal year 1992, federal excise taxes on tobacco generated more than $5 billion in revenue and state excise taxes, $6 billion. An additional $1.6 billion in revenue came from state sales taxes on tobacco. Yet, cigarette taxes in the United States are lower than in many other countries (table). Moreover, while there have been three federal excise tax increases on cigarettes since 1983, taxes as a percent of the average retail price for a pack have declined dramatically—from 47 percent in 1970 to only 30 percent in 1993, while tobacco company profits rose sharply.

Federal alcohol taxes brought in nearly $5.7 billion in government revenue in 1989, but these taxes have been raised only twice on beer and wine and three times on spirits since 1951. If the federal tax on liquor had been adjusted for inflation from 1951 on, a bottle of scotch today would cost an additional $5.50.

State and local alcohol taxes brought in more than $7 billion in 1987. State alcohol and tobacco tax rates vary widely (Indicators 17 and 18), and the two often are not related. Wisconsin, for example, has a heavy cigarette tax and a low beer tax.

Do these taxes pay for the burden that cigarettes and alcohol inflict on society? Economists compared total tobacco and alcohol taxes paid in the late 1980s with the total costs these products imposed upon society—including injuries, medical care, and disability: Cigarette taxes covered societal costs, but alcohol taxes did not. The societal cost of alcohol was more than double alcohol tax revenues.

TABLE

CIGARETTE TAXES: INTERNATIONAL COMPARISONS

	Tax as a percent of price
Denmark	85%
France	76
India	75
United Kingdom	75
Brazil	74
Germany	72
Canada	69
Japan	60
Thailand	54
United States	30

SOURCES

Brown LR and Kane H. *More Countries Raising Cigarette Taxes to Cut Health Care Costs.* Worldwatch Institute Vital Signs Brief #7. *May 26, 1993. Adapted from Table 1.*

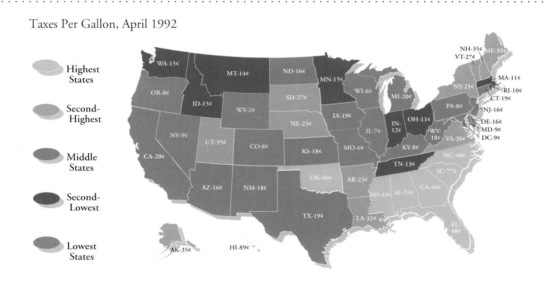

17. State Cigarette Excise Taxes

Taxes Per Pack, January 1993

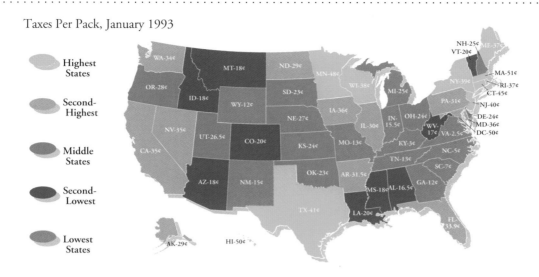

Highest
States

Second-
Highest

Middle
States

Second-
Lowest

Lowest
States

WA-34¢ MT-18¢ ND-29¢ MN-48¢ NH-25¢ VT-20¢ ME-37¢
OR-28¢ WI-38¢ MI-25¢ NY-39¢ MA-51¢
ID-18¢ WY-12¢ SD-23¢ RI-37¢ CT-45¢
NV-35¢ IA-36¢ PA-31¢ NJ-40¢
UT-26.5¢ NE-27¢ IL-30¢ IN-15.5¢ OH-24¢ DE-24¢ MD-36¢ DC-50¢
CA-35¢ CO-20¢ KS-24¢ MO-13¢ WV-17¢ VA-2.5¢
KY-3¢ NC-5¢
AZ-18¢ NM-15¢ OK-23¢ AR-31.5¢ TN-13¢ SC-7¢
MS-18¢ AL-16.5¢ GA-12¢
TX-41¢ LA-20¢ FL-33.9¢
AK-29¢ HI-50¢

18. State Beer Excise Taxes

Taxes Per Gallon, April 1992

Highest
States

Second-
Highest

Middle
States

Second-
Lowest

Lowest
States

WA-15¢ MT-14¢ ND-16¢ MN-15¢ NH-35¢ VT-27¢ ME-35¢
OR-8¢ WI-6¢ MI-20¢ NY-21¢ MA-11¢
ID-15¢ WY-2¢ SD-27¢ RI-10¢ CT-19¢
NV-9¢ IA-19¢ PA-8¢ NJ-16¢
UT-35¢ NE-23¢ IL-7¢ IN-12¢ OH-11¢ DE-16¢ MD-9¢ DC-9¢
CA-20¢ CO-8¢ KS-18¢ MO-6¢ WV-18¢ VA-26¢
KY-8¢ NC-48¢
AZ-16¢ NM-18¢ OK-40¢ AR-23¢ TN-13¢ SC-77¢
MS-43¢ AL-53¢ GA-48¢
TX-19¢ LA-32¢ FL-48¢
AK-35¢ HI-89¢

SOURCES

17. *The Tobacco Institute.* Tax Burden on Tobacco: Historical Compilation. *Vol. 27. Washington, DC, 1993. p. viii.*

18. *Research Institute of America, Inc.* State and Local Taxes: All States Tax Guide. *New York, NY, 1992. p. 271.*

RESTRICTIONS ON ALCOHOL USE

ALTHOUGH ALCOHOL IS a legal substance, many federal, state, and local regulations restrict its use.

Certain activities related to alcohol use are against local laws, such as driving while under the influence (DUI), public drunkenness, disorderly conduct and liquor law violations (Indicator 19a). The number of arrests for alcohol offenses peaked in the early 1980s, with about 3.7 million annually (Indicator 19b). In 1990, there were 3.2 million such arrests. Fluctuations may be explained in part by changes in state and local laws or enforcement practices.

DUIs have increased steadily as a fraction of all alcohol-related arrests, from just over one-third in 1981 to 43 percent in 1991. In most states, DUI offenders will have their driver's licenses revoked or suspended for a period of time. Some states require them to participate in an alcohol education, treatment or counseling program before their licenses can be reinstated. The determination of DUI usually is based on either a specified blood alcohol concentration (BAC) or a sobriety test. In most states, it is illegal to drive with a blood alcohol level at or above 0.10 percent. The *Healthy People 2000* objective is to reduce the legal BAC level for drivers ages 21 and older to 0.04 percent and for younger drivers to 0.00 percent.

Alcohol in any quantity is a risk factor for young drivers, and nearly 40 percent of 16- to 19-year old drivers in alcohol-involved fatal crashes had BAC levels under 0.10 percent. States with lower legal BAC levels for drivers under age 21 have seen significant decreases in traffic fatalities among young people. All states already restrict access to alcohol to anyone under age 21, but enforcement is uneven.

Many states hold the sellers or servers of alcohol partly liable for alcohol's consequences—for example, if they sell to an intoxicated person who is subsequently involved in a traffic crash. These laws have increased bartenders' awareness about alcohol intoxication and boosted participation in server training programs.

19a. Types of Arrests for Alcohol Offenses, 1991

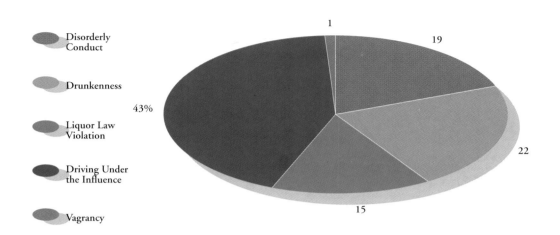

- Disorderly Conduct
- Drunkenness
- Liquor Law Violation
- Driving Under the Influence
- Vagrancy

43%
1
19
22
15

19b. Arrests for Alcohol Offenses Over Time

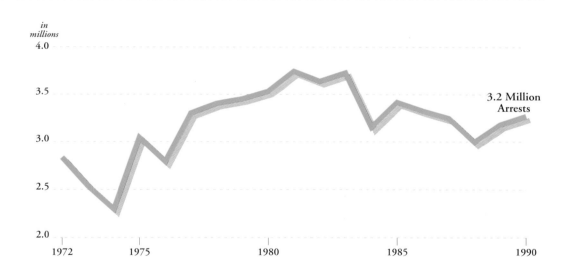

in millions

4.0

3.5

3.0

2.5

2.0

3.2 Million Arrests

1972   1975   1980   1985   1990

NOTES

19a. *"Driving under the influence" includes impairment due to alcohol or any type of drug.*

19b. *Conservative estimates of alcohol arrests because arrests are classified under the primary offense, not whether alcohol was* *involved. Alcohol offenses include driving under the influence, liquor law violations, disorderly conduct, and vagrancy. 1991 data are incomplete at this reporting date and are not shown here.*

SOURCES

19a. *US Department of Justice, Bureau of Justice Statistics.* Crime in the United States 1991. *Washington, DC, 1992. Table 38, p. 223.*

19b. *US Department of Justice, Bureau of Justice Statistics.* Sourcebook of Criminal Justice Statistics 1991. *Washington, DC: USGPO, 1992. Table 4.28, p. 468.*

RESTRICTIONS ON SMOKING

NUMEROUS REGULATIONS CONTROL the sale, marketing, and use of tobacco products. Cigarette advertising on television and radio, for example, was discontinued more than two decades ago, and several states restrict cigarette advertising on state or local government property, including buses, transit stations, and sports facilities.

Almost every state prohibits the sale of cigarettes to underage youth. In nearly all states the minimum age of sale is 18. These laws, however, are inadequately enforced. A 1989 national survey reported that there were 2.6 million current smokers ages 12 to 17, and over half said they usually buy their own cigarettes. While this practice was most common (66.6 percent) among 16- and 17-year old smokers, nearly half of younger smokers also were able to buy their own cigarettes.

Underage smokers buy cigarettes more often in smaller stores (Indicator 20). About 20 percent of smokers ages 12 to 15 purchase cigarettes from vending machines, compared to 12 percent of older teens. Some locales have ordinances requiring a locking device on cigarette vending machines, which retailers are supposed to release at the time of purchase and presumably question the age of the purchaser, but many merchants do not comply. Minors still buy cigarettes from locked machines nearly half the times they try. Colorado and several municipalities in other states have banned cigarette vending machines, and more than a dozen states restrict the placement of machines so that purchases can be monitored.

Smoking bans—partial or total restrictions on public smoking—have been adopted by 46 states, the District of Columbia and about 500 municipalities. These laws range from prohibiting smoking in some settings, such as school buses or elevators, to comprehensive clean indoor air laws that limit or ban smoking in public buildings, restaurants, education and health facilities, retail stores and private worksites. The states with few or no restrictions are concentrated in the South, and those with the most extensive restrictions are in the East and North Central states (Indicator 21). The intent of these clean indoor air laws is to reduce discomfort and health hazards among nonsmokers, but they also may encourage smokers to quit. A *Healthy People 2000* public health objective is to enact comprehensive clean indoor air laws in all 50 states.

20. Where Teen Smokers Purchase Cigarettes, 1989

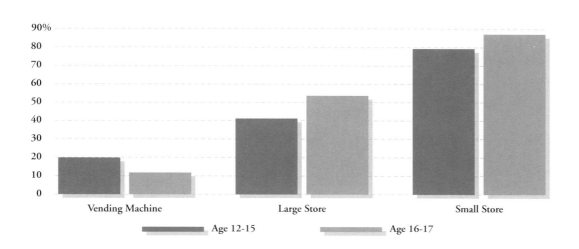

Age 12-15   Age 16-17

21. State Restrictions on Smoking in Public Places, 1992

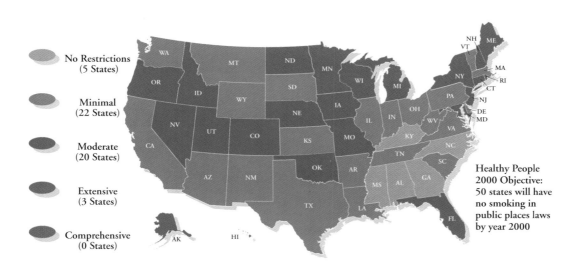

No Restrictions (5 States)

Minimal (22 States)

Moderate (20 States)

Extensive (3 States)

Comprehensive (0 States)

Healthy People 2000 Objective: 50 states will have no smoking in public places laws by year 2000

NOTES

21. Minimal: Some areas have written smoking policy requirements but no minimums are mandated or that designated smoking areas are required in some public places. Mod-erate: Likely to include a few bans and many manda-tory designated areas. Must have restric-tions in most cate-gories to achieve this designation. Exten-sive: Would include bans at least in buildings with possi-bly some designated areas where all agree that smoking can be permitted. Compre-hensive: Bans in almost all areas.

SOURCES

20. *US Centers for Dis-ease Control.* Morbidity and Mortality Weekly Report. *Vol. 41, No. 27. July 10, 1992.*
21. *Coalition on Smok-ing or Health.* State Legislated Actions on Tobacco Issues. *Wash-ington, DC, 1992.*

ALCOHOL AND DRUG ABUSE TREATMENT

ORE THAN 18 MILLION people who use alcohol and 5 million who use illicit drugs are in need of substance abuse treatment. "Need" is determined by consumption patterns and the seriousness of the associated consequences. Overall, less than one-fourth of those needing treatment get it—either due to lack of available space or funding, or because users don't admit they do need it.

Most of the funding for specialty drug and alcohol treatment facilities comes from federal block grants and state and local government funds. Private insurance, Medicaid, and other public insurance programs contribute less than a third of the total funding. In virtually all other areas of medical care, insurance pays the lion's share.

Substance abuse treatment is effective for many people and can decrease the use of alcohol and drugs and increase employment. For some people, brief interventions can be effective, while others require more intensive services and sometimes multiple rounds of treatment. The key to effective treatment is to match individual clients with the intervention most appropriate for them—something too rarely done.

On any given day, more than 800,000 clients receive alcohol and/or drug treatment in a specialized substance abuse treatment program (Indicator 22a). In 1991, most clients—82 percent—were outpatients. Only 8 percent were in long-term residential programs or therapeutic communities. After alcohol, the primary drug of abuse for people in treatment is cocaine or its derivative, crack, followed by heroin and other opiates (Indicator 22b). Polydrug use is common among people in treatment.

Alcohol and drug treatment services also are provided by family practitioners, internists, psychiatrists, and other medical specialists and in emergency rooms. Physicians in these settings can provide early intervention and refer patients to specialized treatment facilities when necessary.

The criminal justice system also renders alcohol and drug abuse treatment. Many people enter community treatment as a condition imposed by the court or criminal justice system, including DUI arrestees. However, less than 10 percent of people in prison receive substance abuse treatment—far fewer than the proportion of offenders with alcohol and drug problems.

Self-help groups such as Alcoholics Anonymous and Narcotics Anonymous are part of the recovery process for many individuals with substance abuse problems. Due partially to the philosophy of the groups to preserve participants' anonymity, accurate counts of current or former members or their current status are not available.

22a. Clients in Alcohol or Drug Specialty Treatment, 1991

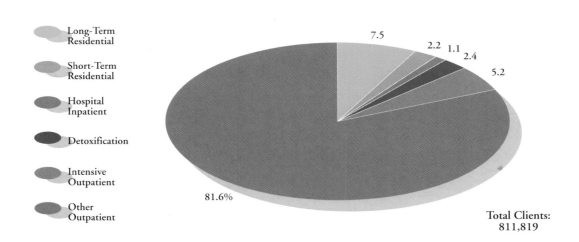

Long-Term Residential
Short-Term Residential
Hospital Inpatient
Detoxification
Intensive Outpatient
Other Outpatient

7.5 2.2 1.1 2.4 5.2

81.6%

Total Clients: 811,819

22b. Principal Drug Used by Clients in Specialty Treatment, 1990

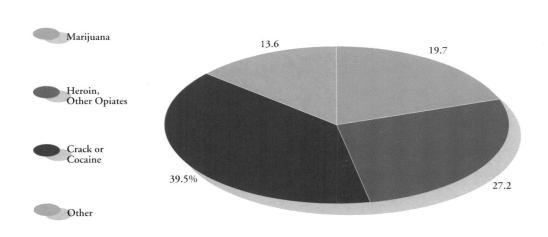

Marijuana

Heroin, Other Opiates

Crack or Cocaine

Other

13.6   19.7

39.5%   27.2

NOTES · **SOURCES** · · · · · · · · · · · · · · ·

22a. *Clients in treatment on September 30, 1991. Forty-five percent of clients were in treatment for alcoholism, 29 percent for drug abuse, and 26 percent for both.*

22b. *Treatment in facilities that offered drug only and combined drug and alcohol treatment.*

22a. *US Substance Abuse and Mental Health Services Administration, Office of Applied Studies.* Highlights from the 1991 National Drug and Alcoholism Treatment Unit Survey. *Rockville, MD. 1992. Table 3, p. 4.*

22b. *US National Institute on Drug Abuse.* 1990 Drug Services Research Survey. Phase 1 Final Report: Non-Correctional Facilities. *Institute for Health Policy, Brandeis University. Waltham, MA. 1993. Table 33.*

SMOKING CESSATION PROGRAMS

AT SOME POINT in their lives, the majority of the 46 million adults in the United States who smoke have wanted to quit. Quitting is difficult, and most smokers initially try to quit on their own but are rarely successful. The most effective way to get people to stop smoking and prevent relapse seems to be to employ multiple interventions and provide continuous reinforcement.

The two basic types of smoking cessation methods are: self-help strategies and assisted strategies. The majority of successful quitters (90 percent) have used self-help techniques, such as quitting abruptly ("cold turkey") or relying on how-to manuals or over-the-counter drugs. One-year abstinence rates for people using self-help methods range from 8 to 25 percent. Assisted strategies include smoking cessation clinics, hypnosis, acupuncture, nicotine patches and other methods involving counselors, physicians, or other health care providers. The cessation rates for people using these strategies are somewhat higher and range from 20 to 40 percent. Nicotine patches are a particularly popular method, with sales topping $880 million in 1992.

Smoking cessation programs are promoted in many worksites. About two-thirds of American companies and most state health departments offer smoking cessation programs to their employees. The most common workplace programs are educational-based, such as providing quit-smoking literature and employee wellness programs (Indicator 23). About one-third of employers sponsor in-house programs to quit smoking or reimburse workers for participating in such programs. Based on company assessments, the most effective programs are cash rewards to workers who quit, employee wellness programs and reimbursement for participation in outside programs.

An important component of many effective smoking cessation programs is a physician who can provide face-to-face advice, set target quit-dates, reinforce smoking cessation and monitor nicotine replacement in conjunction with behavioral interventions. Counseling by doctors, dentists and other health care providers can be instrumental in getting people to quit smoking, or to never smoke at all. Nevertheless, only 47 percent of current male smokers and 54 percent of current female smokers recall that they were ever advised to quit by a physician (Indicator 24). While this is a significant increase since 1966, when only 17 percent of smokers recalled being advised to quit, physicians need to counsel all their tobacco-using patients—particularly people in high-risk groups, such as pregnant women and adolescents. A *Healthy People 2000* public health objective is to have 75 percent of primary care and oral health care providers routinely counsel their patients who smoke to quit.

23. Workplace Measures to Encourage Workers to Quit Smoking

Percent of Workplaces that Tried Measures

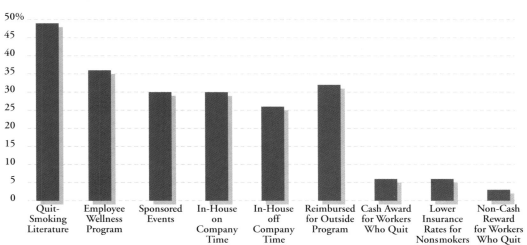

24. Doctors Fail to Advise Patients to Quit

Percent of Smokers 21 and Older Who Recall Being Advised by Doctor to Quit

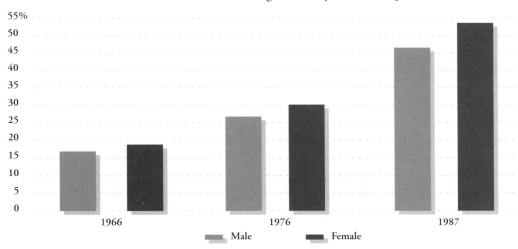

NOTES · · · · · · · · · · SOURCES · · · · · · · · · · · · · ·

24. *Data for 1966 from Adult Use of Tobacco Survey. Data for 1976 and 1987 from National Health Interview Survey.*

23. *The Bureau of National Affairs, Inc.* SHRM-BNA Survey No. 55, Smoking in the Workplace: 1991. Bulletin to Management: BNA Policy and Practice Series. *Vol. 42, No. 34-Part II. August 29, 1991. Table 10, p. 14.*

24. *US Centers for Disease Control.* The Health Benefits of Smoking Cessation. *Rockville, MD: DHHS Pub. No. (CDC) 90-8416, 1990. Table 7, p. 610.*

FURTHER READING

PUBLIC ATTITUDES

Maguire, K, Flanagan, TJ (eds.). *Sourcebook of Criminal Justice Statistics, 1991.* U.S. Department of Justice, Bureau of Justice Statistics. Washington, DC: USGPO NCJ-137369, 1992.

DRUG CONTROL

Reuter, P. Hawks Ascendant: The Punitive Trend of American Drug Policy. *Daedalus: Journal of the American Academy of Arts and Sciences.* Summer, 121(3):15-22, 1992.

PREVENTION AND EARLY INTERVENTION

Klitzner, M, Fisher, D, Stewart, K, Gilbert, S. *Early Intervention for Adolescents.* Pacific Institute for Research and Evaluation. Princeton, NJ: The Robert Wood Johnson Foundation, 1992.

Join Together: A National Resource for Communities Fighting Substance Abuse. *A National Study of Community-Based Anti-Drug and Alcohol Activity in America.* Boston, MA: 1992.

ALCOHOL AND CIGARETTE TAXES

Flewelling, RL, Kenney, E, Elder, JP, Pierce, J, Johnson, M, Bal, PG. First Year Impact of the 1989 California Cigarette Tax Increase on Cigarette Consumption. *American Journal of Public Health,* 82 (6): 867-869, 1992.

Manning, WG, Keeler EB, Newhouse JP, Sloss, EM, Wasserman, J. *The Costs of Poor Health Habits.* Cambridge, MA: Harvard University Press, 1991.

RESTRICTIONS ON ALCOHOL USE

National Institute on Alcohol Abuse and Alcoholism. *Alcohol and Health.* Seventh Special Report to the U.S. Congress. DHHS Pub. No. (ADM) 90-1656, 1990.

RESTRICTIONS ON SMOKING

U.S. Centers for Disease Control. *Reducing the Health Consequences of Smoking: 25 Years of Progress.* Rockville, MD: DHHS Pub. No. (CDC) 89-8411, 1989.

ALCOHOL AND DRUG ABUSE TREATMENT

Gerstein, DR, Harwood, HJ (eds.). *Treating Drug Problems. Volume I.* Institute of Medicine, Committee for the Substance Abuse Coverage Study/Division of Health Care Services. Washington, DC: National Academy Press, 1990.

Institute of Medicine. *Broadening the Base of Treatment for Alcohol Problems: Report of a Study by a Committee of the Institute of Medicine, Division of Mental Health and Behavioral Medicine.* Committee for the Study of Treatment and Rehabilitation Services for Alcoholism and Alcohol Abuse. Washington, DC: National Academy Press, 1990.

SMOKING CESSATION

U.S. Centers for Disease Control. *The Health Benefits of Smoking Cessation.* Rockville, MD: DHHS Pub. No. (CDC) 90-S416, 1990.

CONCLUSION

SUBSTANCE ABUSE: *The Nation's Number One Health Problem* documents the devastating impact that smoking, alcohol abuse, and illicit drug use have on our society. Millions of Americans and their families are affected—young and old, men and women, rich and poor, and rural, suburban, and urban residents. Substance abuse causes illness, death, injuries, school problems, family break-up, and crime. It strains our health care system, as well as our education, social service, and criminal justice systems. It saddles our economy with a tremendous, unnecessary burden.

Many trends are disturbing. Although overall consumption is down, frequent heavy use is relatively unchanged. Mortality related to substance abuse remains high and is increasing dramatically for drug-related AIDS deaths.

Drug-related crime continues to grow.

Fortunately, some positive signs are evident. For example, awareness of the health risks associated with substance abuse is increasing, and the public is growing more intolerant of abuse. Overall use of tobacco, alcohol, and illicit drugs is down. Motor vehicle fatalities involving alcohol are decreasing.

As a nation we seem to be doing better in combatting the problem of substance abuse. At least some prevention, intervention, and treatment activities are in place in most communities across the country. These activities are increasing, as more people become committed to fighting substance abuse in their community, their city, their state, and their country. The trends noted in this report will provide benchmarks for assessing the impact of their efforts.

INDEX